Getting to know you –

Defending the Faith

C.Brian Ross

Vol 3 in the "Getting to know you ..." series

By the same author:

Great Words of the Faith (Vol.1 in the "Getting to know you ..." series).

Foundations of the Faith (Vol.2 in the "Getting to know you ..." series).

All Scripture quotations, unless otherwise indicated, are taken from the Revised Standard Version of the Bible, ©1952 [2nd edition, 1971] by the Division of Christian Education of the National Council of the Churches of Christ in the United States of America. Used by permission. All rights reserved.

All rights reserved. No part of this publication may be reproduced, stored in a retrieval system, or transmitted, in any form or by any means, electronic, mechanical, photocopying, recording, or otherwise, without the prior written permission of the author.

ISBN: 9781791394387

Printed in the U.S.A.

© Copyright 2018.

Introduction

Getting to know you –

The Letters from John

It was in July, 1976 that, as the recently inducted minister of Bellshill Parish Church, in Lanarkshire, Scotland, I attended the annual Keswick Convention in the beautiful English Lake District. The Bible Readings were given, that year, by the Rev Eric Alexander – at that time minister in Loudoun East Parish Church, Newmilns, in the Covenanting district of Ayrshire. He gave those readings, on I John, over four sessions of about one and a half hours each.

Mr Alexander was no stranger to me, as he was a good friend of Rev George B Duncan – my own former minister in St. George's-Tron Parish Church, Glasgow – and had occasionally been a guest preacher before that congregation. Knowing that I was going to receive good, solid, teaching I went along with a new notebook, and took a lot of notes on each morning.

As the new winter session approached, I had already decided that I wanted my evening worship service in Bellshill to be a teaching service. Deliberating on what I should do to achieve this end, I decided to use the notes taken at Keswick as the basis for a full series of messages on I John. I wrote to Mr Alexander to ask if I was at liberty to do so, and received a very gracious response in the affirmative.

Decades later, having been called to live, and serve, in S.W. France, I was asked if I would bring some teaching to a group of anglophones who deemed that they were not receiving sound Biblical teaching elsewhere. I was specifically asked if I would teach from I John, so the notes were taken down from a shelf, and edited for a new group of people, in a new situation.

It is the notes for that second series, with some additional new material, that is the basis for this book. It is not intended to be a scholarly commentary – others are much better qualified to produce such a volume; and many have done so. However, having commenced as a series of messages to an ordinary, working-class, congregation; and having been revised to meet the needs of a group of "ex-pats" in France; it is my hope and prayer that, in this book form, it will be helpful to ordinary people, who may not have received much beyond a secondary education, but who wish to understand better what "the beloved disciple" had to say to the church some nineteen centuries ago – and how his words may relate to us in the early decades of the 21st century.

Acknowledgements

As with my previous literary efforts, thanks are due to a number of people. Obviously, Eric Alexander is at the top of that list! Had it not been for those Keswick Bible Readings, I might never have looked, seriously, at the wonderful letter that we know as I John. I also wish to thank Tilsley College, Motherwell for allowing me access to their Library whenever I was in Scotland. I was delighted that Eric Alexander was willing to endorse this publication – and, of course, am grateful to the others who have done so. In a publication of more than 50,000 words, there are bound to be typographical errors, and I am grateful to Margaret Ollivier, and my own dear wife, for having taken the time to proofread the document. Any remaining mistakes – in spelling, grammar, or theological content – are entirely my own responsibility.

Once again, my wife has put up with my temporary disappearances into my study as I spent many hours "slaving over a hot keyboard" and I thank her for her unfailing patience!

However, as always, the deepest thanks must go to the One Who has guided me throughout my life, and Who has provided me with the education, ability, and desire to "publish abroad His wonderful Name" – even the Covenant God Who is the God of Abraham, of Isaac, and of Jacob, and Who is the God and Father of the Lord Jesus, the Christ to Whom, with the Father, and with God the Holy Spirit, be all honour, and glory, and praise, now and throughout eternity.

Gardonne, 2018

"I warmly commend this excellent piece of work from the pen of Brian Ross on the New Testament Letters of John. There are three characteristics of the work which are admirable. First, it is expository in its intention: the author's concern is to explore what the text of Scripture teaches. Secondly, it is applicatory in its form: that is, the truth is applied to Christian life and behaviour. And finally, it possesses clarity in its structure. I would expect it to have a wide uptake throughout the Christian church."

Rev. Eric Alexander
Formerly minister in St George's-Tron Parish Church, Glasgow.

"This is a very readable book, and I would happily have it available to hand out to encourage people to understand, more deeply, their need to speak out their faith to those amongst whom they live."

Rev. Dominic Stockford,
Minister, Christ Church, Teddington.
Chairman, The Protestant Truth Society

"In *Defending the Faith* Brian Ross takes us through the three letters in the New Testament, penned by the "beloved disciple", the elderly apostle, John. He deals in I John with, among other things, the need for disciples of Jesus to be aware of false teaching - specifically the Gnostic heresy; the importance of fellowship; and the need to grow in the faith. In II John, he draws out the apostle's warning against false, itinerant, teachers while, in the third of the letters, he shows that John commends hospitality, and condemns a spirit of control in the church. Brian writes, as does John, from a pastor's heart."

The Venerable Dr Paul Vrolijk
Senior Chaplain and Canon Chancellor
Archdeacon of North West Europe

Table of Contents

Setting the scene 1

1. Recall to Fundamentals 9
2. The Fellowship of Faith 21
3. Walking in the Light of God 37
4. Knowing I am His 55
5. Growing in the Faith 67
6. Developing as a disciple 81
7. Family characteristics 95
8. Being "in the family" 113
9. Love – the major characteristic of the family 127
10. The confidence of the child of God 143
11. The nature, and character, of Almighty God 159
12. The three tests, and the new life 173
13. Assurance! 183
14. The disciple's experience 200

Appendices

II John and III John

Introduction 215

A warning against itinerant deceivers 219

The spirit of control 233

x

Setting the scene.

John, the beloved disciple

Whilst there are no contradictions between the two main writers of New Testament documents – Paul and John – there are some distinctive differences. Paul is the great expounder of doctrine; the revealer of the mystery of salvation by grace, through faith (Eph.2:8); and the explainer of the purposes of Almighty God for the Church – the Body of the Lord Jesus, the Christ. John, on the other hand, brings greater depth to our understanding of the Person of the Lord Jesus; of the basic truth that Almighty God, the Creator and Sustainer of all that exists, is Light and Love; and of how these divine characteristics should deeply affect all that disciples of the Lord Jesus are, and do.

John outlived all of the other members of the apostolic band. It is perfectly conceivable that he was little more than a teenager or, at most, in his early twenties, when he began to follow Jesus of Nazareth. He lived, and worked, with Jesus for three years – and spent the rest of his life reflecting on that period, and walking in the light of Jesus as revealed by God the Holy Spirit. He was, of course, one of those closest to Jesus, and is generally accepted as being

> *"That disciple whom Jesus loved ..."* (John 21:7, *inter al*)

He was especially blessed by being granted

> *"The revelation of Jesus Christ, which God gave him to show to His servants what must soon take place;"* (Rev.1:1).

John, it would appear, spent many years at the end of his life in the area around Ephesus and, around about 90 AD, he wrote his account of the Gospel record, and the three letters that are the subject of this volume. At some point, he was a prisoner exiled to the Greek island of Patmos in the Aegean Sea where, by 95 AD, and allegedly in a cave, he received and wrote down the Revelation. The cave is now a popular pilgrimage site. He died of old age some time during the reign of the Emperor Trajan (98-117 AD).

Although this book does not deal with John's record of the Gospel, it is worth noting that, in that record, he deals primarily with the dual nature of the Saviour – His humanity and His deity. John's record stands apart from the other three – the Synoptic records of Matthew, Mark, and Dr. Luke. For example, it starts with a deliberate allusion to Genesis 1, rather than with the birth, or baptism, of the Christ. It contains the Master's statements of Self-revelation: the seven "*I am*"s –

> "... *the Bread of Life*" (6:35);
>
> "... *the Light of the world*" (8:12);

"... *the Door*" (10:9);

"... *the Good Shepherd*" (10:11);

"... *the Resurrection and the Life*" (11:25);

"... *the Way, the Truth, and the Life*" (14:6);

"... *the Vine*" (15:5).

It is John who, in his Gospel record, reveals the heart of the Lord Jesus through His prayers – chapters 11, 12, and 17; and who focuses on the teaching that Jesus gave His disciples prior to His crucifixion – chapters 13-16.

The Letters of John were written in the context of false teaching that was already infiltrating the Church. We shall look at some of these teachings as we go through the First Letter, but they include, for example, the false teaching that Jesus had not come in the flesh (I John 4:2-3). This was the heresy known as "Docetism" (from the Greek word that means "to appear"). It taught that Jesus only <u>appeared</u> to be a man. Indeed, in its extreme form, it taught that, when He walked on sand, He left no footprints!

Another heretical teaching was that Jesus' atoning sacrifice on the cross was not necessary for the forgiveness of sin (I John 5:6-7), thus diminishing the "blood" symbol (see Heb.9:22) of His cruel physical suffering and literal death.

There were also people then, as now, who professed to have a relationship with Almighty God, through Jesus the Christ, without displaying evident obedience to His commands, submission to His Word, or the fruit of the Spirit.

So the aged apostle wrote a series of letters:

- I John – to counteract false teaching;
- II John – to a local church so that they would not receive false teachers into their fellowship;
- III John – to a key brother who was in the habit of providing hospitality to itinerant teachers, in order to encourage him to receive some genuine teachers of the truth who were in need of his help, and also to warn him about a self-centred leader named Diotrephes.

These letters bring a challenge to 21st century disciples of Jesus. That challenge is to maintain the correct balance between protecting the local fellowship of believers from false teaching, without disassociating ourselves from those who may not believe exactly the same as us, on things that are not of the essence of the faith. It is to learn to fellowship with those who bring the message of God that challenges us and enables us to move forward as a local manifestation of the Body of the Christ, accepting change and development without losing the core of what it means to be genuine followers of the Lord Jesus.

In recent (or, perhaps, not so recent!) years, there appear to have been two specific dangers that the Church has faced. The first of these is liberalism – the down-playing of the divine nature of God's written Word. This has led to some who have claimed to be "ministers of the Gospel of the Lord Jesus, the Christ" denying His deity, His atoning sacrifice, His uniqueness as the only way to the Father. These, of course, are some of the heresies with which John had to deal pastorally. Truly,

> "... *there is nothing new under the sun.*" (Eccles.1:9)!

Another danger is what we might refer to as "exclusivism" – the failure to recognise, love, and relate to, the whole Body of the Christ; all true followers of Jesus. Rev. David A. Robertson, of St Peter's Free Church of Scotland in Dundee, was Moderator of the Free Church Assembly in 2015. In his moderatorial address he issued a plea that we recognise, and seek "… to encourage and help all our fellow Christians in Scotland. Whether it is those who remain within the C of S, or those who don't share our specific Reformed theology but nonetheless are 'most in the main things', let us love and support our brothers and sisters. I have enjoyed working with Charismatics such as those associated with CLAN even though there are some things I struggle with. We find the brothers and sisters of Christ in many unexpected places. One of my favourite McCheyne quotes is - *"I would rather have pastor Martin Boos, preacher of the Church of Rome, though he was, preach in my own pulpit, than some frigid evangelical from my own church"!"*

The Lord Jesus made two statements that, at first sight, may appear to be contradictory! Of course, as we look at them closely, we discover that they are not. They are simply two sides of one coin. They are:

"... *he that is not against you is for you.*" (Lk.9:50)

– in other words, be inclusive; embrace all of those whom Jesus embraces as His own.

"*He who is not with Me is against Me, and he who does not gather with Me scatters.*" (Lk.11:23)

– in other words, be alert for error, and reject it, even although this will mean disassociating from some people. This is also part of John's teaching, as we shall discover.

John provides us with five specific purposes for writing his first letter. These are:

- that there may be complete joy among all believers – 1:4;
- that there may be purity of life (holiness) – 2:1;
- that the 'commandment of love' may be the primary working principle in all of our relationships – 2:7;
- to identify and deal with false doctrine – 2:21, 26;
- that all believers may have the assurance of their salvation, and of the eternal life that it brings – 5:13-15.

He also identifies evidences of a genuine Christian faith – of being a true disciple of Jesus:

- walking in the light – 1:6;

- obeying the commands of Jesus – 2:3, 5:2;
- Christ-likeness (becoming increasingly more like Jesus) – 2:6;
- displaying love towards fellow-believers – 2:9, 3:10 & 14;
- displaying love towards God – 5:2;
- not habitually sinning – 3:6-10, 5:18;
- being anointed of God shown by the evident presence of God the Holy Spirit – 3:24, 4:13;
- having correct doctrine regarding the Person and work of Jesus, the Christ – 4:1, 5:1;
- experiencing victory over the world – 5:4.

So, with that general overview, let us commence our look at these letters, and seek to know them better, that we may be encouraged, and that He may be glorified in our lives.

Chapter 1

Recall to Fundamentals

In the Introduction, I have acknowledged my personal indebtedness to the Rev Eric Alexander for his Keswick Convention Bible Readings of 1976, that provided the basis for a series of messages, on I John, that I then brought to the congregation of Bellshill: St. Andrew's Parish Church, Lanarkshire.

I didn't then, and don't now intend to, spend any time going into the theories of some liberal theologians concerning the authorship of the letter; the identity of its recipients; or the location of its origin. This is intended to be more of a devotional commentary than a critical study, and such matters are dealt with, more than adequately, elsewhere. Suffice it to say that it is generally agreed that this letter was written by John, the beloved disciple (see John 21:20), the author of the fourth of the Gospel accounts; and that it was written in Ephesus to the groups of disciples of Jesus for whom John had pastoral responsibility.

The letter neither begins, nor ends as we might expect from other New Testament letters. It has neither the opening, nor the closing, greeting of the letters from Paul. Yet, as Prof.

Barclay states, it is a letter with an "intensely personal character." In it, John is concerned, as a pastor, with the well-being of those entrusted to his care, and the whole letter betrays this concern for the spiritual health of the members of the family of God. It was probably written against the Gnostic, heretical, teaching that was all too common in the first couple of centuries of the Christian Church – and which has never completely disappeared. The two particular teachings that were common to all of Gnosticism were:

(a) That matter is inherently evil – a doctrine that affected their belief in the Incarnation, and in the doctrine of sanctification; and
(b) That knowledge is everything – that salvation is merely a process of enlightenment, unrelated to morals or ethics.

Eric Alexander, in his first Keswick Reading, suggested that the letter is like a spiral staircase that, while going over the same ground time and time again, rises ever higher; or, like a musical symphony in which the basic themes are stated, and then repeated and expanded until they build up into the full and perfect symphony.

The main themes that he suggested we would find are:

(a) Right obedience to God;
(b) Right love for one another; and
(c) Right belief of truth.

This we will discover to be true as we proceed through this volume. In this chapter, we look at just the first verse, and the challenge that it can bring to us.

If there is going to be fellowship, there must first be faith and, in this verse, John reveals how faith came into his own heart and life. It is, we might say, his personal testimony and, if this is the way in which faith came into the heart and life of John, then surely there will be lessons that we may learn, as to how that faith can come into our hearts and lives, and how we may ensure that it comes to others.

> *"That which was from the beginning, which we have heard, which we have seen with our eyes, which we have looked upon and touched with our hands, concerning the Word of life –"*

John begins this letter as he does his account of the Gospel, by setting it in the context of eternity. Here is no passing fancy, but something

> *"… which was from the beginning,"*

Another point of similarity to his Gospel record is his reference to "the Word" as a description of the Lord Jesus. This is, of course, a very suggestive title for words reveal what is in the mind, and what is in the heart.

I recall the story of a minister who was attending a weekend Conference. On the Friday evening, one young woman gave a glowing testimony of her journey to faith in the Lord Jesus. Everyone was suitably impressed. The next morning, the minister turned a corner and, accidentally, bumped into the same young woman who was obviously in a hurry. Out of her mouth came a foul expletive. Then seeing who it was into whom she had bumped, she apologised. The minister looked at her with sadness in his eyes. "Ah, my dear," he responded, "it's only when a glass is knocked that the true contents spill out!" The Lord Jesus, the Christ, reveals and expresses what is in the mind, and heart, and character of Almighty God, the Father.

Whether, or not, that incident really took place I cannot confirm. However, I also recall working with a man whom I barely knew, on an old Mini that had been left in a garage for some twelve years. At one point, as I was pounding at a seized-up piston with a heavy hammer, I missed the piece of wood that was transferring the force of the hammer to the piston, and hit my thumb instead! "Aaowhh! That hurt", I exclaimed. My co-worker looked at me. "You really are a Christian!" he exclaimed. "If I had done that, you would have heard a mouthful!" Sadly, he also professed to be a follower of Jesus!

Now, using polite language at all times does not make one a Christian – there is much more to it than that. However, it cannot be denied that, if you hear profanity, crude language, and/or blasphemy, emanating from my mouth, you have every right to question the validity of my claimed faith!

John uses three mighty phrases. He speaks, first of all, of

"That ... which we have heard."

In this phrase, we are reminded of the declaration that the Gospel must have. Prof. Barclay writes, "What men are interested in is not someone's opinions and speculations and ingenious guesses, but in a word from the Lord." There must be an audible, a vocal, communication. This was what had sparked off John's experience. He had listened to what Jesus had to say; was arrested by it; and, finally, was convinced by it. So we find, in the experience of John, on his way to saving faith, there is a primacy given to the spoken word.

This, of course was one of the central aspects of the Reformation – the 500th anniversary of which is being celebrated in this year in which I have commenced putting this book together – with its five "Solae" principles:

1. Sola Scriptura – Scripture alone;
2. Sola Fide – Faith alone;
3. Sola Gratis – Grace alone;
4. Solus Christus – Christ alone; and
5. Soli Deo Gloria – to the glory of God alone.

The old system of the Roman church, in which the basis of everything was the liturgy and the sacraments, was cast aside for, important 'though such things may be, they can only exist at all by virtue of the Word. So, in everything from ecclesiastical architecture, to the regular order of service, the Reformers gave the Word the primacy that it had always deserved. They placed the pulpit in a focal position in the church building; they made the sermon to be the climax of the service of public worship.

And how desperately we need to recapture this realisation – that if people are going to believe in Jesus, the Christ; if they are going to place their trust in Him, and in Him alone; if they are going to commit themselves fully to Him; they must hear about Him, and know about Him.

Writing to the disciples of Jesus in Rome, Paul, quoting from the writings of the Old Testament prophet, Joel, said that:

> "… *every one who calls upon the Name of the Lord will be saved.*" (10:13)

But then he goes on to ask:

> "*But how are men to call upon Him in whom they have not believed? And how are they to believe in Him of whom they have never heard? And how are they to hear without a preacher?*" (10:14)

The spoken Word, the preached Word, has a vital place in bringing unbelievers to the point of faith. Turning again to Prof. Barclay, he writes of "a great teacher [who] always used to tell his students that their one aim as preachers must be 'to speak a good word for Jesus Christ'."

> "… *And how are they to believe in Him of whom they have never heard? And how are they to hear without …*"

someone 'to speak a good word for Jesus Christ'?

But if this is so – and I am firmly convinced that it is – then there are certain points that we must note concerning the spoken word. First of all, we must note that the audience for the message must be secured. So much of what we say; so much of our preaching; never reaches those for whom it should be meant. Sunday by Sunday, all over the world, ministers, pastors, vicars, priests, so-called "lay-preachers", preach the Gospel message – but they do so with in the walls of their particular building for congregational worship, be it a mighty cathedral, or a prefabricated mission hall. However, to a very large extent, they are preaching to people who have already heard the Gospel message hundreds of times before!

But those people who seldom, if ever, enter a church building, also need to hear the Good News that

> "... *in Christ, God was reconciling the world to Himself,*" (II Cor 5:19);

the Good News that guilty man can be proclaimed righteous in God's sight, through the inestimable sacrifice at Calvary. So, either these people must be brought into the church, or the church must take the Gospel message to the people – wherever they are!

This is a simple, even an obvious, fact; but one that many disciples of Jesus, never mind those who are merely "nominal" Christians, have totally failed to grasp. There simply must be an audience secured for the preaching of the Word of God. And the responsibility for this rests, not upon the leadership, but upon the people – everyone who claims to be a member of the Body of the Christ. All of us, every single disciple, has a responsibility towards others – a corporate responsibility – to spread the Gospel message to them. However, that responsibility rests upon us as individuals.

When my wife and I were members of St George's-Tron Parish Church, in the city of Glasgow, under the ministry of the late Rev. George B. Duncan, the church had a monthly Guest Service. The object was that members of the congregation would invite their friends to come to the worship service just as they would invite them to come to their homes. But, of course, any disciple of Jesus should be able to do this at any time! This is just one way of ensuring that an audience for the message is found.

Then, of equal (if not greater!) importance, is the taking of the Gospel message to where others are. I attended a minsters' conference, many years ago, when one of the speakers, in a series on "Communicating with Youth", stressed the need for the Gospel to be verbalised and vocalised. We simply must open our mouths and speak; telling others of this wonderful Jesus Whom we claim to follow. This is why I have my blog, in which I frequently share some Gospel truth, while also posting on other topics of interest. It's why I involve myself in online discussions – with unbelievers!

An audience for the message is essential; but we must also be careful to ensure that the message, itself, is accurate.

In II Cor. 5:20, Paul writes, concerning disciples of Jesus that

> "... *we are ambassadors for Christ.*"

And one of the many requirements for an ambassador is that (s)he pass on any message from the Head of State exactly as it has been received. So we are neither to change the message, nor to invent a new one. We are to proclaim that which has been given to us –

> "... *the faith which was once for all delivered to the saints.*" (Jude 1:3).

Now this means that the truths of God have to be learned; otherwise God the Holy Spirit Who is, Himself, the Spirit of Truth (John 15:26, *inter al*), will not own that which we speak, or preach. I never fail to be amazed at the number of people who profess to be disciples of Jesus, will go to so much trouble to learn, for example, a new hobby; but that so few will seek to learn anything about the faith that they profess to hold! This was my original reason for preaching the series of messages on which this book is based – and other, similar, series – that those who came to those evening diets of worship would have the opportunity to gain some knowledge of God's Word, and use it to His glory. It is, as a friend here in France often says, ignorance of the Word that is at the seat of many of the difficulties that the church faces in these end times.

Of course, as F. F. Bruce points out, "Neither theology nor morality is necessarily the worse for being 'new'. When our Lord began His public ministry in Galilee, His hearers recognised that what He brought was 'a new teaching' (Mark 1:27); and those who listened to the Sermon on the Mount were aware that they were being presented with a 'new morality', ..." (The Epistles of John, P&I, Glasgow; 1970. p.26). However, we must be careful that the "newness" does not obscure the intrinsic message of the Gospel.

But not only must we learn the truths of God; the very tone of voice that we use when communicating those truths must be in keeping with the character of God. How often I misrepresent the Gospel of the grace and love of God by the manner of my speech – even if the content of my message is Biblically sound! The Gospel is "Good News" – yet it may be proclaimed in tones of abysmal gloom! It is the message of the grace, and love, and power, and peace, of God and, as such, it ought to bring a glow to our faces, and a smile to our lips.

There must be an audience for the message; we need to ensure that the message is delivered accurately, and winsomely; and we need to declare the message with authority.

We read of the Lord Jesus that

> "... *He taught them as One Who had authority, and not as their scribes.*" (Matt.7:29; Mark 1:22).

And here we are directed to the Person and ministry of God the Holy Spirit. When I first preached through I John, it was not untrue to say that He was the most neglected Persona[1] of the Godhead. It is still true to say that we dare not, and must not, take Him for granted. Because, ultimately, He alone is

---

[1] See my book "Great Words of the Faith"; chapter on The Trinity.

the One Who can bring anyone to faith in the Lord Jesus. But He must have lives that He is able to use; lives through which His authority and power may operate.

This, of course, is a monopoly that must be respected. The work of both conviction and conversion is something that we are not asked to do. It is something that, Jesus said, God the Holy Spirit would do. He will convict of sin through the ministry of the apostles and disciples. "He will expose the naked truth that the root of sin lies in the desire of men to live their lives in self-centred independence, disowning any allegiance to Jesus." (R.V.G.Tasker; Tyndale N.T. Commentary, 1970; *in loc;* cf. John 16:8). Jesus also made clear that those who are His disciples are

"... *born of the Spirit.*" (John 3:8).

It doesn't happen as often now, but there was a time when I would regularly have someone say to me, in a somewhat jocular manner, concerning a friend or colleague: "Here's someone for you to convert!" My invariable reply was "But that's not my job! Only God the Holy Spirit can do that. My job is simply to bring people to meet with Him; to explain to them their need of salvation; and to leave the rest to Him!"

The story is told of, I believe, the great American evangelist, D.L. Moody that, while walking in a town in which he was conducting an evangelistic campaign, he came across a drunk man, literally in the gutter. The man, in spite of his inebriated state, recognised the evangelist.

"Mr Moody," he said, "I'm glad to see you. I'm one of your converts!" D.L. Moody looked at him, with sadness. "That, sir," he replied, "is obvious. You are certainly not one of the Holy Spirit's!"

Of course, it is possible for you, or for me, to restrict the ministry of God the Holy Spirit. Paul warns us:

> "*... do not grieve the Holy Spirit.*" (Eph.4:30);

and we grieve Him when we fail to allow Him to do in us, and be in us, that for which He has been sent.

A declaration that the Gospel must have. Are you playing your part in declaring it; in securing an audience for it; in stressing its accuracy; in showing its authority?

If you're not, is it because you don't have the faith that John had? And if not, why not? It's yours, just for the asking, given freely by Father God, in the Christ, through the indwelling of God the Holy Spirit.

God grant that we might be able to say, with John:

> "*That which was from the beginning, which <u>we</u> have heard ... concerning the Word of life.*"

Chapter 2

The Fellowship of Faith

John's first letter is not as much a traditional letter as a sermon sent out to the fellowships for which the aged apostle carried pastoral responsibility. In the previous chapter, we discovered that there is a declaration that the Gospel message must have – this Gospel message that is the Good News about Jesus, the Christ (and which **is** Jesus, the Christ). We saw that there is an illustration that the Gospel must have – you and I, who profess to be disciples of Jesus, need to reflect that in our daily lives as we display the love and compassion towards others that we see in the life of the Lord Jesus. Finally, we recognised that there is an examination that the Gospel will stand. We need to live our own lives, aware that we are being watched – by a world that, while cynical and sceptical, is also hungry and thirsty for the satisfaction that in fact, only God, in Christ, can provide! In other words, we thought on the Gospel as it is presented audibly, visually, and tangibly – and were challenged, I hope, as to whether, or not, we are presenting it in a similar manner to those around us, that they might be brought to the same saving faith in the Lord Jesus that John had, and that I believe each of us has; that we and they might tread the same pathway together. However, that faith is not an end in itself! It produces what John refers to as fellowship; and that is our theme in this chapter. So let's look at the next few verses:

> "... - *that which we have seen and heard we proclaim also to you, so that you may have fellowship with us; and our fellowship is with the Father and with his Son Jesus Christ. And we are writing this that our joy may be complete. This is the message we have heard from him and proclaim to you, that God is light and in him is no darkness at all."*

All too often, people will claim that one can be a perfectly good disciple of Jesus without ever going near a church building, or being part of a group of like-minded people. However, in the Scriptures, the Christian experience is never portrayed as being lived in isolation. It is always shown as being in relationship to other disciples of Jesus – as well as to Father God.

> "... *let us consider how to stir up one another to love and good works, not neglecting to meet together, as is the habit of some, but encouraging one another, and all the more as you see the Day drawing near."*
> (Heb. 10:24-25).
>
> "*Two are better than one, because they have a good reward for their toil. For if they fall, one will lift up*

> *his fellow; but woe to him who is alone when he falls and has not another to lift him up. Again, if two lie together, they are warm; but how can one be warm alone? And though a man might prevail against one who is alone, two will withstand him. A threefold cord is not quickly broken."* (Eccl. 4:9-12).

> *"… the Lord appointed seventy others, and sent them on ahead of him, two by two, into every town and place where he himself was about to come."* (Luke 10:1).

Another common fallacy, even within church circles, is that we are all God's children: "We're a' Jock Thamson's bairns!" to use a familiar Scots saying. This is the fallacy that we are all one great big family of mankind; a brotherhood of man!

According to God's own Word, this is not so. In the prologue to his account of the Gospel, John writes:

> *"He [i.e. Jesus] came to His own home, and His own people received Him not. But to all who received Him, who believed in His Name, He gave power **to become** children of God; who were born, not of blood nor of the will of the flesh nor of the will of man, but of God."* (John 1:11-13; *emphasis added*).

In other words, I am not a child of God by nature; I have to be**come** a child of God! And, in order to do that, I need power. And that power only comes when I accept that I am a sinner; that I can do nothing about my own sinfulness; that only Almighty God can do anything about it; and that He has done what was needed, in the Persona of the Son as He hung on a cross outside Jerusalem, bearing **my** sins, in **His** Body, on that tree. I respond to that, with repentance, and in faith, receiving Him into my life; handing my whole life over to His control. Or listen to Paul, writing to the early disciples of Jesus in Rome:

> "... ***all who are led by the Spirit of God*** *are sons of God.*" (8:14; *emphasis added*).

I am a child of God, a member of His family, when I am led by God the Holy Spirit.

My physical birth made me a part of God's creation; one of His creatures; and that I do have in common with all of mankind throughout all of history. But it was my spiritual birth; that being "*born again*" of which Jesus spoke to Nicodemus; that made me a child of God, adopted into His family; able to claim all of His riches in Christ Jesus; able to call Him "Father"!

It is fellowship within that family of God; fellowship among those who can call God "Father"; that is John's theme in these verses. With this in mind, we may note the design that fellowship has.

How is it made up? What are its constituent parts? When I come to the point of faith in the Lord Jesus, how do I move on to fellowship? How is fellowship expressed in real terms?

In v.3, John informs us that all that he has already written concerning the eternal, and the historical, nature of the Gospel, is proclaimed

> *"... so that you may have fellowship with us; and our fellowship is with the Father and with His Son Jesus Christ."*

So, there are two sides to fellowship – the manward side, and the Godward side. Or, if you like, fellowship operates in two directions – vertically and horizontally, or upward and outward.

The late John Stott, arguably one of the most influential Anglican clergymen of the last century, and former rector of All Souls, Langham Place, writes: "Fellowship is a specifically Christian word, and denotes that common participation in the grace of God, the salvation of Christ, and the indwelling Spirit, which is the spiritual birthright of all Christian believers. It is their common possession of God – Father, Son, and Holy Spirit – which makes them one. So", he goes on, "John could not have written "... *that you may have fellowship with us;"* without adding *"and our fellowship is with the Father and with His Son Jesus Christ."*, since our fellowship with each other, arises from, and depends on, our fellowship with God." (Tyndale Press Commentary; p.63).

The Amplified Version of the Bible offers this expansion of v.3:

> "*And this fellowship which we have (which is a distinguishing mark of Christians ...*"

So how about you, and me? Do we know real fellowship with other members of the particular group with which we identify as our "congregation"? Do we have a real spiritual relationship with them? If not, then perhaps the first thing that ought to be checked on is our own relationship with Father God; the reality of our fellowship with Him! Because that's where it starts!

"But how", you may respond, "do I recognise this fellowship? How is it expressed?" Someone has described fellowship in the Christian life as being similar to a game of tennis. One person serves the ball over the net; the other player returns it; and so the game is played. We would think it absurd if someone wanted to just stand there, demanding that others serve to him, while he made no effort to return the play! Whatever else might be happening in such a bizarre situation, it is absolutely clear that a game of tennis would not be being played!

So, fellowship is expressed in sharing and reciprocating. It has been defined as "a living intercourse between personalities". Father God has opened the game by manifesting Himself, supremely, in the Lord Jesus, and thus bringing into being this living intercourse with His children.

We must continue the game by, as it were, playing among ourselves.

The design that fellowship has – a vital sharing relationship between one true child of God and another; and between all true children of God, and their heavenly Father. Is this the fellowship that we enjoy? Or is the extent of our 'fellowship' what John Stott described as "a superficial social camaraderie"?

Not that there is anything at all wrong with social relationships and activities. However, if they take the place of a genuine spiritual relationship with other believers, and with Father God Himself, then there is, I would contend, a serious problem.

But let's move on to consider the delights that fellowship brings.

Just in case anyone comes to the conclusion that, just because this fellowship of which John writes is a spiritual fellowship, it must be dull and boring, he goes on to say:

> *"And we are writing this that our joy may be complete."* (v.4).

The words *"our joy"* in the RSV and most other translations, are translated *"your joy"* in the AV and a few other translations! Both translations of the Greek are, in fact, perfectly possible, and each makes perfect sense! However, the NEB almost certainly captures the true sense of what John intended when it provides us with

> "... *we write this in order that the joy **of us all** may be complete.*" (*emphasis added*).

What a tremendously important place joy has in the New Testament – both in the purpose of God and in the life and experience of the disciple of Jesus! But what, exactly, is the form of that joy that is to be associated with fellowship? Surely it may be seen in two ways – first of all in the joy of sharing with others.

Some may recall the old adage – "A sorrow shared is a sorrow halved; a joy shared is a joy doubled." And this is at least part of the joy of genuine Christian fellowship. It may be Father God sharing His thoughts with me as I read His Word during my private devotions; or me sharing my hopes, and desires, and fears, with Him as I pray. At the human level, it may be a sharing, between believers, of a problem, or a burden; or of some discovery that we have made in God's Word, or some experience we have had of God's grace. But, whatever it is, to have someone with whom to share it increases that joy – or halves the sorrow in other situations. Of course, halving sorrow could be viewed as amounting to the same thing as increasing the joy!

Such sharing is both enriching and encouraging as we discover, perhaps, that we are not alone in having a particular problem, and as we share with others the way is which God has been dealing with us, and with them. The joy of sharing with others, and then there is the joy of serving with others.

One of the best ways of deepening fellowship, at the human level, is to do something together. I recall my own early Christian life – Boys' Brigade, Christian Endeavour, Summer Mission. There was a real joy experienced in a common service of Jesus.

Paul, writing to church in Corinth, assured them that

"... *we work with you, for your joy* ..." (II Cor 1:24).

It's always a joy to serve the Lord – but to do so alone is rarely as meaningful as to find others alongside, sharing with us, and we with them; praying together; witnessing together. As a student at the Bible Training Institute in Glasgow, in the late 1960s, I and my fellow students were involved in various aspects of practical work. We would go to our allotted area of the city and go from door to door, seeking to present the Gospel in one way or another. And we always went in pairs! During the summer between my two years of study, I spent a month in the Black Isle area in the north-east of Scotland, involved in colportage. This meant that, in the days before Amazon was anything other than a South American river, we went from door to door offering Bibles and other Christian literature for sale. But the Scottish Colportage Society ensured that we went in pairs!

There is, of course, good Biblical warrant for this course of action. We read of Jesus that:

> "... *He called to Him the twelve, and began to send them out two by two,*" (Mark 6:7);
>
> "*After this the Lord appointed seventy others, and sent them on ahead of Him, two by two ...*" (Luke 10:1).

I have no doubt in my own mind, that all who have experienced that level of fellowship would readily testify to sheer thrill of it!

John, then has something to say about the design that fellowship has; about the delights that fellowship brings; and, finally, in this short section, we can see something of the demands that fellowship makes.

> "*This is the message we have heard from Him and proclaim to you, that God is light and in Him is no darkness at all.*" (v.5).

"*God is light*" and, throughout the Scriptures, we find that light has to do with truth, and righteousness, and purity. It follows, therefore, that if you and I are going to have fellowship with Almighty God or, indeed, with His true children, we must meet certain requirements, or demands. There are, for example, demands in the realm of the mind.

I must be willing to submit my mind to the truth of God; to yield the way in which I think to what He has revealed in His Word. The darkness that is the opposite, and absence, of light is the darkness of ignorance – lack of knowledge – that can breed despair. But do you remember the words of the aged Simeon when Mary and Joseph brought the infant Jesus to the Temple – words that have become part of the liturgy of the church in their Latin form: the Nunc Dimittis? Luke records – probably what he learned from the lips of Mary herself – that Simeon:

> "... *took Him up in his arms and blessed God and said, 'Lord, now lettest Thou Thy servant depart in peace, according to Thy word; for mine eyes have seen Thy salvation which Thou hast prepared in the presence of all peoples,* **a light for revelation to the Gentiles, and for glory to Thy people Israel**.*'"* (Luke 2:28-32; *emphasis added*).

And, of course, the coming of the Lord Jesus was described, prophetically, in those well-known words form the writings of Isaiah:

> *"The people who walked in darkness have seen a great light; those who dwelt in a land of deep darkness, on them has light shined."* (Isa 9:2).

Jesus came in order to dispel the darkness, and ignorance, about the very personality of God. He came to be

> *"the light of the world"* (Jn.8:12; 9:5),

and fellowship with Him demands that I accept the truth of God, and be willing to act upon it. We must remember, too, that He also said to His disciples:

> *"You are the light of the world. A city set on a hill cannot be hid. Nor do men light a lamp and put it under a bushel, but on a stand, and it gives light to all in the house. Let your light so shine before men, that they may see your good works and give glory to your Father Who is in heaven."* (Matt 5:14-16).

It follows from all of that that there will also be demands in the moral realm.

Not only my attitudes are involved, but also my actions. That's why Jesus can be pointed to as a great moral teacher. He is that – although He is much, much more. And He has set ethical standards for His followers to attain. Not, of course, that we must be perfect before we can have fellowship with Him, because no mortal will ever be perfect and, indeed, not even the righteousness that we have before God is our own, but is imputed to us in, and by, the Lord Jesus!

Some people seem to live as the Gnostics I mentioned in the previous chapter, who saw the spirit as pure, and the body (being material) as evil. They deduced from that that it didn't matter what happened to the body; how it was used; how it was abused. Now it is true that, as Paul wrote to the disciples of Jesus in Galatia that:

> *"It was for freedom that Christ set us free;"* (5:1)

However, although we have liberty in the Christ, we must be careful that we do not slip into licence!

"When a person becomes a Christian, it doesn't mean he is free to be a criminal. It does mean that the Christian does not need to be controlled or restrained by the 'walls of the law'. He is controlled by internal restraints built in by the ministry of the Holy Spirit. The rules have not changed; God's moral standards remain the same. But the person who becomes a Christian needs no external restraints. His obedience is produced internally by the Holy Spirit." (John MacArthur Jr.; "Galatians", p.95).

We must, at the very least, have a holiness that has been described as "if not a matter of attainment, then at least a matter of aspiration in our hearts and lives." We must be in the company of those who

"hunger and thirst for righteousness" (Matt.5:6).

We must be

"pure in heart" (5:8),

even 'though our lives fall far short of that ideal.

The late Dr Paul Rees spoke at a conference I attended, many years ago. He told the story of a small boy who was sitting in garden making mud pies. His dad returned home from work, sat down exhausted in the heat, and said "I'm so thirsty"! The boy immediately got up and went, dirty little hands and all, and filled a tumbler with cold water. His muddy little hands smeared the exterior of the tumbler as he carefully carried it back and, in order to ensure that he didn't let it fall, he hooked a small dirty finger over the top – with the tip dipping into the water, and the mud washing off and slowly sinking to the bottom. Dr Rees' comment was: "That was perfection of intention, if not of achievement!"

In similar vein, I still recall helping my paternal grandmother to bake some bread. Well, what happened was that she gave me a small piece of bread dough and a small oval baking dish. I had just come in from the garden and, as I kneaded my piece of dough, its lovely whiteness was gradually replaced by a dirty grey! I must have had some notion of hygiene, because I realised that this was unsatisfactory and, going through to the scullery, I washed it and dried it – with a not too clean dishcloth and towel! I then baked it and, when my dad arrived home from work, presented it to him. In an object lesson on a father's love, he accepted my "offering", and ate every last crumb!

As a still relatively young student at Teacher Training College, my Principal Teacher on my first teaching practice, constantly offered me what she referred to as "the counsel of perfection"! It is questionable as to whether, or not, I ever attained such a lofty height – but the intention was always there!

There is a moral demand that we have to face if we are going to have fellowship with Father God and, through Him, with all of His people – and it is a demand that we cannot ignore!

Fellowship within the family of God – the design it has; the delight it brings; the demands it makes. Is it a fellowship of which you and I are part? Is it a fellowship of which we want to be part? Are we prepared to meet the whole will of God for His children; His will for us as individuals; that we may have fellowship with Him, and with one another? God grant us the needed grace that it may be so – to the glory of His most holy Name.

Chapter 3.

Walking in the Light of God

So far, as we have looked at I John, and in just the first few verses, we have discovered that there is a declaration that the Gospel message must have – this Gospel message that is the Good News about Jesus, the Christ (and which **is** Jesus, the Christ). We saw that there is an illustration that the Gospel must have – you and I, who profess to be disciples of Jesus, need to reflect that in our daily lives as others as we display the love and compassion towards others that we see in the life of the Lord Jesus. We recognised that there is an examination that the Gospel will stand. We need to live our own lives, aware that we are being watched – by a world that, while cynical and sceptical, is also hungry and thirsty for the satisfaction that, in fact, only God, in Christ, can provide!

We have also learned a little bit about fellowship – that shared participation in the grace of God, the salvation of Christ, and the indwelling Spirit, which is the spiritual birthright of all Christian believers; that is their common possession of God – Father, Son, and Holy Spirit – which makes them one. We learned about the design it has: a vital sharing relationship between one true child of God and another; and between all true children of God, and their heavenly Father. We noted the delight it brings – in sharing with others, and in serving with others. But we also realised that there are demands that it makes – in the mental realm, and in the moral realm.

In this chapter, I want to look at a slightly longer section of John's letter: 1:5 – 2:2.

> *"This is the message we have heard from him and proclaim to you, that God is light and in him is no darkness at all. If we say we have fellowship with him while we walk in darkness, we lie and do not live according to the truth; but if we walk in the light, as he is in the light, we have fellowship with one another, and the blood of Jesus his Son cleanses us from all sin. If we say we have no sin, we deceive ourselves, and the truth is not in us. If we confess our sins, he is faithful and just, and will forgive our sins and cleanse us from all unrighteousness. If we say we have not sinned, we make him a liar, and his word is not in us.*
>
> *My little children, I am writing this to you so that you may not sin; but if any one does sin, we have an advocate with the Father, Jesus Christ the righteous; and he is the expiation for our sins, and not for ours only but also for the sins of the whole world."*

"When I want to judge a man" (not very 'politically correct'!), someone has said, "I don't go by what he says, but by what he does." And this is so true – what I say is, all too often, belied by my actions! You may remember the old adage: "Actions speak more loudly than words". Or, what about: "I can't hear what you are saying, for watching what you are doing"?

It's clear that our Christian life; our lives as disciples of Jesus; must be more than just talk. We need to be walking the talk – and being seen to be doing so!

John is very much aware of this. He had obviously been disturbed by reports he had received of false teaching in these churches for which he had pastoral responsibility, and he writes these words to refute what these false teachers were promoting as true Christian doctrine.

Three times in this passage John uses a recognisable formula – the first part to do with speech; the second with action.

"if we say ... but if we"

and then comes the very opposite. He refers to those who make all sorts of false claims – words that fail to be backed up by action; words that are, indeed, outright heresy; teaching that is contrary to what God has revealed in His written Word, and through His Son – the Word made flesh. It may be that he is alluding to actual slogans of the false teachers but, if not, he is certainly representing their pernicious teaching – which he then goes on to brand as deceitful error.

He starts off with one of the great theological statements of the letter:

"*God is Light*"

and underlines it with the negative

"*and in Him is no darkness at all*".

Light has many properties. It reveals. It pervades everything unless it is deliberately blocked out. To John, the ultimate test is whether, or not, a person's teaching is backed up by their behaviour; and whether, or not, both can stand the examination of the One Who is Light – and not the feeble glimmer of a matchstick, but the piercing brightness of a laser beam!

We have a great enemy – sin (and the satan who is the producer, and instigator, of sin). Nine times in this section, John refers to sin, and he illustrates his theme by contrasting light and darkness. God is Light; sin is darkness.

All three of the errors with which John deals in this passage are concerned with sin – the fact of it in our conduct; its origin in our nature; and the consequences of it with regard to our relationship with Father God. Speaking of these errors, John Stott writes: "They are the misconceptions of men who want fellowship with God on easy terms. They have never learned the indissoluble marriage of religion and ethics; they are seeking a divorce between them. They have a thoroughly inadequate doctrine of sin and its sinfulness in relation to God, Who is Light." (*op.cit.; in loc.*)

As we look at these erroneous teachings, we find that they still have their exponents today. But we also find that, in each case, John also gives the divine remedy. The three false claims that the heretics were making show a progression of thought. First, there is the man who does not recognise the darkness, i.e. the lack of fellowship with God in which he lives. He is followed by the person who claims perfection at any given moment, and finally, there is the one who denies that he has ever sinned or shown any of its imperfections.

We begin with the claim:

> "*If we say we have fellowship with Him while we walk in darkness, we lie and do not live according to the truth;*" (1:6)

This is the denial that sin breaks our fellowship with God. We must note that "walk" in this Scriptural context refers to all of moral conduct. What was being taught, by the Gnostic heretics, was that "it is possible to have fellowship with God, while leading an immoral life"!

We have already noted that one of most important beliefs in Gnosticism was that the body is a mere vehicle for use by the soul and the spirit. Just as if I allow my car to rust, it doesn't affect my person, so – they taught - nothing that happened to the body had any effect on the spirit. They believed that "if a man had become truly 'spiritual' he had progressed beyond the possibility of any defilement. 'You could', they said, be righteous without necessarily doing righteousness' and, consequently, spiritual communion with God was independent of physical morality." (*Stott; op.cit., p.74*) "You can be righteous without acting righteously.", they taught. "You can have spiritual communion with God independent of physical morality"!!

By that name, Gnosticism is a thing of the past. But its descendants are still around and, in these last days, once again proliferating. Sadly, as in John's day, many in positions of Christian leadership – claiming fellowship with Father God through the Church of the Lord Jesus, but seeing no necessity to come to the foot of the Cross for cleansing and forgiveness, and then to seek to lead, by His grace, lives consistent with their profession!

I recall once, having occasion to go through a congregational Communion Roll (in the Church of Scotland). Every so often was written beside a name: "Not interested". At one particular place, there was a later addition: "Deceased". I was not trying to be unkind/cynical when I commented "She's interested now – but too late!" Someone who appears to have walked in spiritual darkness; not even sufficiently interested to attend the worship services: but who, while claiming to be a member of a local congregation was, as such, according to the confession made, and the vows taken when entering membership, claiming to be a member if the Body of Christ!

To say that such a union is even possible, says John, is to lie! There is no other way of putting it. Because

> *"God is Light"* –

and light and darkness cannot exist together.

However, having refuted the error, the apostle goes on to affirm the related truth:

> *"… but if we walk in the light, as He is in the light, we have fellowship with one another, and the blood of Jesus His Son cleanses us from all sin."* (v.7).

He is speaking, here, of our living in the light and the presence of God. Spending every moment with Him; sharing every matter with Him. And, says John, there will be two results of such a walk.

First of all, we

> *"have fellowship with one another"*.

It's true that the corollary of walking in darkness which is hindering fellowship with God, is that walking in the light would enable us to enjoy fellowship with God! But John, whilst in no way denying that, takes it a stage further. He looks back to what he has written in our v.3, and the implication that while each of us has fellowship with God then, with Him (if I may put it like this with all reverence) as a sort of Common Denominator, we have fellowship with one another!

But the second result of walking in the light is that

> *"the blood of Jesus,* [God's] *Son cleanses us from all sin."*

This assures us that Father God not only forgives my sins, and my sinfulness; but that He also erases them completely! This is not to say that He "forgets" them. As the Almighty, Omnipotent, Creator of all that exists, He does not forget. However, as God, He is able to "not remember". In other words, He does not hold our sins against us (cf. II Cor.5:19).

Some of us may recall, in pre-Word Processing days, the use of a duplicator. The 'high tech' of the 70s! A special sheet – a 'skin' – was placed in a typewriter. If I made a mistake in my typing – a regular occurrence! – then I painted over the offending letter with a special fluid that, effectively, formed a new skin. So I was able to start again, with an unmarked skin – a clean sheet! The mistake was no longer there. And the particular tense that John uses in the Greek language in which he wrote his letter, shows that this cleansing, and renewing, of which he speaks is a continuous process. As I walk, I am continuously cleansed, as every failure is immediately brought into the searing beam of God's righteousness. But that laser-like beam is itself tempered by His love, shown in the means by which the cleansing is provided – even

> *"the blood of Jesus, His Son."*

John Stott sums up his comments on these verses by writing: "The condition of receiving cleansing through the blood of [the] Christ, and of enjoying fellowship with each other, is to walk in the light; to be sincere, open, honest, transparent." Is that a description of your life, and mine? If not, then God's Word – not Brian Ross! – says that we are walking in darkness: spiritually, morally, or both! And if that is the case, then we cannot honestly say that we have fellowship with Him, and all our show of religion is sheer hypocrisy!

So, the first false teaching with which John deals is the denial that sin breaks our fellowship with God. But these heretics went a stage further! Their first claim at least appeared to acknowledge the existence of sin, while denying that it affected our relationship with God. But then they went on to the denial that sin exists in our nature!

"we have no sin"! (v.8).

They were denying the very inherited principle of self-centredness; what the theologians refer to as "original sin". They were saying, in effect, that "whatever their outward conduct may be, there is no sin inherent in their nature". (Stott; op.cit., p.77). They were claiming to have reached that state of sinless perfection that some, even today, claim to have attained.

Yet even such a disciple of Jesus as Paul wouldn't make a claim like that. Writing to his fellow-believers in Rome, he assured them:

> *"I do not understand my own actions. For I do not do what I want, but I do the very thing I hate. Now if I do what I do not want, I agree that the law is good. So then it is no longer I that do it,* **but sin which dwells within me**." (Rom 7:15-18; *emphasis added*).

No doctrine of sinless perfection there! When I was saved, my sin was, as it were, put into the dustbin. Often, however, it manages to get out, and has to be returned. But even if it were the case that it never got out, that wouldn't alter the fact that it is there. Just as our household rubbish is still in the dustbin – or, at least in the bin-bag that is in the small wheelie-bin that we have – until the lorry comes around and the rubbish is tipped into it, so my sin remains until that glorious day when I stand in the nearer presence of the Lord, and am then perfect, because I shall be as He is! (3:2).

So, says John, if, like these heretics,

> *"we say that we have no sin, we deceive ourselves, and the truth is not in us."*

Our friends are not deceived by our protestations of sinlessness – they know us only too well! God is certainly not deceived – he knows us even better! The only one who is deceived is 'self'. And our very self-deception is a sign that the truth is not in us but that we are, rather, being controlled, however subtly, by the devil!

But what is the alternative?

"*If we confess our sins,*"

writes John,

> "[God] *is faithful and just, and will forgive our sins and cleanse us from all unrighteousness.*"

The first thing we must note is not merely the need to confess, but the change from singular to plural! The heretics claimed that they had no sin – John tells us to confess our sins. That plural is significant. Confession must be particular. We need to consciously name our sins before the Father. **We dare not deal with abstractions.**

The proper attitude to sin, for the disciple of Jesus, is not to deny it, but to admit it, in all of its shameful detail, and so receive the forgiveness that God has made possible, in the Christ, and which He has already promised to those who repent. We must acknowledge, before Him, that we are sinners – not only by nature, but also in our practice. But because He is faithful to His own Word; because He is righteous and just; He will forgive – He will absolve from sin's punishment; and He will cleanse – He will absolve from sin's pollution.

The Gnostic heretics may have been teaching, as some do today, a doctrine of sinless perfection. But to John, the only answer to sin was, and is, confession. And not a general confession of sin, but a particular confession of sins, as we deliberately call them to mind, confess, and forsake them. As one of the published prayers of Prof Baillie (a Scots theologian from many years ago) puts it: "Lord, what I thought it not shameful to commit, let me not think too shameful to confess."! And if the confession causes us pain, we should rejoice that our conscience has not been completely deadened, but may still be used by God to keep us in His way! Of course, if such confession can be undertaken glibly, with barely a thought, then we are in serious trouble, and may need to spend much time in prayer, and in the reading of the Word!

The first heresy that these false teachers were propounding was the denial that sin breaks our fellowship with God.

The second was that sin exists in our nature.

And then they go further still with the denial that sin shows itself in our conduct.

"we have not sinned"

was their claim. "We may concede that, in theory, sin would break our fellowship with God if we were guilty of it. We may even accept the possibility that sin does exist in our nature. But we deny that **we** have, in practice, committed sin, and put **ourselves** out of fellowship with God."

This is the ultimate in the teaching of these heretics – and John's reaction is most strong! Claiming to have fellowship with God while walking in darkness may be a lie; claiming that sin is no part of our nature may be deceitful to ourselves; but to actually claim that

> *"we have not sinned"*

is to make a liar out of Father God Himself – and that is blasphemous, and reveals that

> *"His word is not in us"*,

because that Word declares the universality of sin.

> *"there is no man who does not sin"*

said Solomon in his prayer at the dedication of the Temple (I K.8:46). The psalmist wrote:

> *"They have all gone astray, they are alike corrupt; there is none that does good, no, not one"* (14:3).

In Eccles.7:20, the Preacher says:

> *"Surely there is not a righteous man on earth who does good, and never sins."*,

while the word of the Lord through Isaiah was that

> *"We have all become like one who is unclean, and all our righteous deeds are like a polluted cloth"* (64:6).

And, of course, by the time that John was writing, many of Paul's letters would have been in general circulation, not least that great letter to the church in Rome, with all of its deep theological teaching, and its stern reminder that

> *"all have sinned and fall short of God's glory"* (3:23).

Indeed, as John Stott points out, "the word of the Gospel, which is a Gospel of salvation, clearly assumes the sinfulness of man"

But, having made this point, John changes his approach. Instead of going straight to his third "*but if*", he begins a complete new sentence. And, lest anyone think that he was being unduly severe, he begins with the words

>"*My little children …*" (2:1)

words that suggest both the author's advanced age, and the loving relationship that existed between him and his readers.

Then he goes on to make the rather strange statement:

>"*I am writing this to you so that you may not sin …*"

This sounds uncommonly like the very concept of "sinless perfection" that he has just condemned! So what was John thinking?

Perhaps he suddenly realises – or the Holy Spirit, Who was inspiring him, pointed out to him – that what he had just written concerning frank admission, and full forgiveness, of our sins might cause some to think lightly of them; that we might take the path that some take whereby all that we have to do is confess, and then we are free to go and commit the same sin all over again; that as long as I have confessed just before I die, my spirit will go to heaven! This latter, by the way is, to my understanding, the thinking behind the Roman "sacrament" of the last rites!

So John makes clear that his purpose is to prevent sin, not to condone it in any way at all. However, all too aware of the weakness of human nature, and the impossibility of that high ideal being realised, he then brings in his "*but if*" as he says

"*if anyone does sin …*"

And God's remedy is, of course, the Lord Jesus!

John uses a particular description of Jesus. He calls Him our "Advocate". This is a word from the Law Courts, and was used for the one who pleaded the cause for the defence. One day, I will stand before Almighty God. But I will not stand alone. The One Whose blood and righteousness are now my necessary covering, as I approach the throne of grace will, on that day, no longer stand in front of me to, as it were, protect me; but will stand beside me as my righteous Advocate! The One Who, indeed, intercedes for me in my absence will, on that day, say: "Father, this one is mine!"

Finally, in this section, John uses another important word to describe the Lord Jesus. He says that Jesus is

"*the expiation for our sins…*"

Some translations use the word "*propitiation*".[2] The same Greek word is translated by both words from time to time. But there is a slight difference in the terms. Expiation is the act that results in the change of God's disposition toward us. It is what Jesus did on the cross, and the result of that work

---

[2] There is a full chapter on these terms in "Great Words of the Faith".

of expiation is propitiation—God's anger is turned away. The distinction is the same as that between the ransom that is paid, and the attitude of the person who receives the ransom. We might put it simply as meaning that Jesus is the One Who reconciles us to the Father by His sacrificial death on the Cross, that covers over all of our sins, and makes us to be accounted as righteous in the Father's sight. (cf. II Cor.5:19).

And, John assures us, this expiation is

> "... *not for our* [sins] *only, but for the sins of the whole world.*"

Not that all sins are automatically pardoned through the atoning blood of the Christ – that would merely be another way of belittling the gravity of sin, and of cheapening the divine sacrifice – but that a universal pardon is offered for the sins of the whole world, although it is enjoyed only by those who embrace it.

Imagine that I come to a group of friends with a large box of chocolates, and state that I have purchased them for the group and that all may share in them. Most hands are immediately outstretched to receive. However, one person is on a diet, and declines the offer. Now, that person cannot, with honesty, claim that I did not provide a chocolate for him/her. It was their personal decision to not accept that which was offered freely!

John heard the reports of the false teaching in the church. And he refuted it, in each of its aspects, by basing his response on the sacrifice made at Calvary. Many congregations, and fellowships, have a cross as a kind of centre-piece in their buildings. But it's only as we take that cross, with all that it symbolises, to the centre of our lives, that we can meet the false teaching that is so prevalent today. For, even today, there are those who would deny that

> sin breaks our fellowship with God;
>
> sin exists in our nature;
>
> sin shows itself in our conduct.

They may not use those precise terms; they'll make all sorts of excuses; but all that they do is lie, deceive themselves, and make God out to be a liar. But they, like their 1st century counterparts, will receive their own reward!

God grant that none of us be found either among their number, or following their teaching; but let us realise that the Christian life – the life of the disciple of Jesus – is, first of all, confessing/admitting our sins, and our sinfulness; then going to the foot of the Cross for that forgiveness that is offered through the blood of the Christ, and that wipes out the past; and for that cleansing that, by His continued grace, makes the future new.

Chapter 4

Knowing I am His

In the previous chapter, we looked at a difficult passage from John's letter – a passage that even some of the great commentators have acknowledged as being difficult to simplify. Basically, John was pointing out three ways by which it could be seen that a person is not a true disciple of the Lord Jesus, the Christ. Such a person might claim to be one of the Christian fellowship; even a leader/office-bearer in the fellowship; but if that person made the denials of which John wrote – denying that sin breaks our fellowship with God; sin exists in our nature; sin shows itself in our conduct – or even if that person was living those denials without actually uttering the words; then he was, and is, walking in spiritual darkness, and is no child of the Light that is Almighty God Himself.

In the passage at which we look in this chapter, John takes a different tack. In this section, he speaks of assurance. It may have been that he realised that what he had just written could have an unsettling effect. So, as a pastor, he now offers three ways by which I may know that I **am** a true disciple of Jesus!

He begins, in v.3, by stating that

> "… *by this we may be sure that we know Him,*".

This concept of 'knowing God' is one of the central thoughts of the whole letter. But what does John mean by it? Not merely having information regarding God – that would be knowing about Him – but to have entered into a personal relationship with Him; a relationship that is meaningful, and vibrant, and of ultimate importance.

If I were to compare my own wife with, for example, the Princess Royal, the results would be very interesting.

You see, I know quite a bit about the Princess Royal. I know her real name; I know when she was born; know about her marriages – and divorce; I know about her children; I know that she has represented her country in Olympic Equestrian events; I know about her ability to sing *Flower of Scotland*; I know about some of the good work that she does. And what I don't know I could quickly, and easily, find out by doing an online search. However, I have never met Anne; I have never even been in her company; I don't **know her**!

With my wife, the situation is totally different. She is someone whom I know. Oh, I know a lot about her as well – not everything: I am but a mortal man, and which man would claim to know all about any woman, even a wife of now 48 years (and counting!)?! But I do know her. It's a personal knowledge. It's a knowledge that is based on a relationship. It's an intimate knowledge.

I know **about** the Princess Royal; I **know** my wife.

One of first topics on which I had to write at The Bible Training Institute, in Glasgow, was "An encounter with the Christ in the Gospels". Only as we have that personal encounter with the Lord Jesus can we know God, in Him. And, says John, the evidence of this knowledge is obedience:

> "... *by this we may be sure that we know Him, if we keep His commandments. He who says "I know Him" but disobeys His commandments is a liar, and the truth is not in him; but whoever keeps His word, in him truly love for God is perfected.*" (vs.3-5).

There are two trains of thought here, the first of which concerns our loyalty to the Lord.

Sometimes, in preparation I lift, not another translation of the Bible, or some theological tome, but my dictionary – to check on the meaning of a particular word. I liked one of the definitions given for loyalty: "personal devotion to a sovereign". Because, of course, that's where real obedience springs from – devotion. So, our obedience should spring from personal devotion to **the** Sovereign – even the Lord Jesus: He Who is coming again, not as a helpless Babe in a manger, but as King of kings and Lord of lords. (see Rev.19:16).

This is the ultimate distinction between the disciple of Jesus and the unbeliever/heretic – loyalty to the Lord Jesus, the Christ, that is seen in obedience and devotion to Him. It's that important word "commitment". It's perfect obedience. And if any should object that, in that event, no-one knows God because no-one is perfectly obedient, we may reply with the comment of John Calvin that John, here, "... does not mean that those who wholly satisfy the law keep [God's] commandments [and, other than Jesus Himself, no such instance can be found in the world] but those who strive, according to the capacity of human infirmity, to form their life in obedience to God." We might illustrate it by thinking of a video I watched recently of a dance-school that had opened its doors to some children with physical handicaps. The children tried to emulate the other students. They didn't quite manage to do so – but each one deserved an 'A' for effort!

And this is not merely a New Testament concept! It is clear in Old Testament as well. Indeed, the priority of the Sinai Covenant was on obedience to God's laws, and not on the carrying on of complex rituals – as the prophets consistently stated.

Another train of thought, here, concerns the maturity in our love.

> "... *whoever keeps His word, in him truly love for God is perfected.*" (2:5)

If we have the new life that comes through committing ourselves, in faith, to Jesus, then we also have a new love. But that love, like life itself, although it comes to us as a gift, must be allowed to grow and develop into what John later calls

> "*perfect love* [that] *casts out fear*" (4:18);

a love that is marked by a complete and utter confidence in the One Who is loved.

And this love illustrates the great difference between this obedience and the obedience that we give to those who have authority over us in the human realm. Often, **that** obedience is given because we fear the consequences of any disobedience – whether a child fearing the corporal punishment of its parent; or the adult fearing the custodial sentence handed down by a court of law. But this is the obedience of love that desires to keep His commandments; that longs to please Him. And as we obey, more and more, the will of God in our lives, so He will unveil more and more of His mind and will, as He finds us trustworthy.

You want to be assured that you're a Christian; a true disciple of Jesus? John offers this first test – that in the genuine Christian life there is a loyalty to the Lord, and a maturity in your love, that show an obedience that is clear evidence of salvation.

The second test that he gives, by which I may have assurance, concerns not knowledge of God, but union with the Christ. And the evidence of union <u>with</u> the Christ is likeness <u>to</u> the Christ.

> *"By this we may be sure that we are in Him: he who says he abides in Him ought to walk in the same way in which He walked."* (2:5-6).

We have already noted that to "walk" in this spiritual sense, is to do with the whole of life. So what John is saying is that conversion brings about not only knowledge of God, but also union with Him in and through the Christ. And this will, indeed must, affect the character and quality of my life.

Let's note the illustration of the way in which we should live. And that illustration is, quite simply, Jesus Himself – He is to be our great example.

What greater example of obedience could be found? How prominent a part it played in His earthly life! He taught His disciples, in that model prayer, erroneously referred to as "The Lord's Prayer"[3], (actually the disciple's prayer) to pray

> *"Your will be done on earth as it is in heaven"*.
> (Matt.6:10).

He said of His own attitude towards the Father:

> *"My food is to do the will of Him Who sent Me, and to accomplish His work."* (Jn.4:34),

and, again,

---

[3] The true "Lord's Prayer" is found in John 17!

> *"I have come down from heaven, not to do my own will, but the will of Him Who sent Me."* (Jn.6:38).

In the Garden of Gethsemane, He prayed

> *"... not what I will, but what Thou wilt."*, (Matt.26:39)

and, on the Cross, His great shout

> *"Tetelestai"* (*"Finished"*) (Jn.19:30)

spoke of His redemptive work, done in loving obedience to the Father. So it was that Paul, writing to the believers in Philippi, could say of his Lord that He was

> *"... obedient unto death, even death on a cross."* (Phil.2:8).

John saw, in Jesus, a perfect illustration of that obedience of which he had just written, and so presents Him as an illustration of the way in which we should be living if we are saved, and united to Him as branches to the living vine.

But, more than that, John saw an obligation as to how the disciple of Jesus should live. An obligation laid on His disciples by Jesus Himself.

His final words to them, before ascending to right hand of Father, were

> *"... you shall be my witnesses ..."* (Acts 1:8).

That is to say, they – and we, if we are His disciples – are to let others see, and know, of Him both by what we say, and how we live.

I said at the beginning that Eric Alexander had pointed out that this letter may be likened to a spiral staircase, or a musical symphony. The first covers the same ground, time and time again, but always rising to new heights; in the latter, the same theme is stated, but with ever-rising intensity and expansion. Here, we find that we are back to the theme of **showing** the Gospel.

Not every believer has the gift of preaching or teaching. But every one of us ought to be living the Gospel, and thus showing it to those around us. As Francis of Assisi is alleged to have said – although there is doubt about it and, of course, even if true, it isn't the whole story – we should "Preach the Gospel at all times and, if necessary, use words"! And if we are thus living out the Gospel message, then we may be assured that we are His disciples. The two go hand-in-hand! We are not just to know the gospel, and preach the gospel; we are to be living examples **of** the gospel – examples of grace and faith and love. We want our lives to support the gospel, to commend the gospel, to make it attractive to others. We want the words we say about Jesus Christ to be accompanied by the sweet aroma of a Christ-like life. Our behaviour affects the reputation of the message. One bad example can mar thousands of good words, and good works!

A good example, however, helps the gospel to be favourably received. That is one of the dynamics at work in what has become known as "friendship evangelism". People can be won to Jesus in only a few words after they have seen some good examples of the gospel in action. As Paul wrote,

> "*Conduct yourselves in a manner worthy of the gospel of Christ*" (Phil.1:27).

Some behaviours are worthy of the gospel, and some are not. Our example, yours and mine, is important. Our lives should reflect the grace and faith we have in Jesus, the Christ.

Assurance, to John, has not **merely** to do with vocabulary; with saying that we know Him. And it is certainly not a matter in which we can be complacent, for any complacency must surely be shattered the moment we look to Jesus and see in Him the illustration of the life we ought to be living – a life that is constantly witnessing to the union we have with Him.

The evidence of knowledge of God is obedience to Him; the evidence of union with the Christ is likeness to Him; and the evidence of walking in the light is living in love.

This is the third test that John offers by which we may have assurance, and we find it in the longer section: vs 7-11.

He points out, by way of reminder, that what he is writing is no novelty; no gimmick. It is something that his readers have had *"from the beginning"* (v.7).

Yet, it is still wonderfully new, and always will be until the end of time itself.

As some of us used to sing: "The old, old story, it is ever new; the old, old story, praise the Lord 'tis true"

Once again, John is concerned with the walk of the disciple of Jesus; the significance of the way in which you and I live. He notes, first of all, that the Christian life is progressive.

The very idea of "walk" suggests movement; direction, progress. Living the Christian life is like riding a bicycle – if you don't keep moving forward, then you fall off! There can be no such thing as standing still in the life of a true disciple of Jesus – there must always be progress.

One of the heretical ideas that we looked at in the previous chapter was that of 'sinless perfection'. There were those who were claiming that they led sinless, blameless, lives. John's response was straightforward, and simple: "Rubbish!" However, although it is true that, while we remain in these mortal bodies, we will never be sin**less**; we ought, if we are true disciples of Jesus, to be continually becoming less sin**ful**! We should be undergoing that continuous, transformational, process that theologians refer to as sanctification – simply, growing more like Jesus. Prof Barclay often quoted the well-known prayer of Richard, a 13th century Bishop of Chichester, that was popularised in the musical "Godspell":

"O most merciful Redeemer, Friend and Brother,
May I know Thee more clearly,
Love Thee more dearly,
Follow Thee more nearly,
Day by day."

It is the process of sanctification, by the indwelling of God the Holy Spirit, that enables me to do so.

The Christian life is one of progress, in both love and obedience. And each of us must be moving forward. But the Christian life is also productive.

Love, and light, and progress, are all positive, ongoing, subjects. And, as such, they produce positive results. So, if I am in the Light, and progressing in love, my life will have positive results; I will be helpful to others; I will love my brother/sister, no matter who (s)he may be. And, says John, in this situation,

> *"there is no cause for stumbling"* (v.10).

I like the translation in the French Segond 21 version (which, of course, I now translate into English!):

> *"there is nothing that can trip him"*.

It is in the dark that we stumble, and trip over objects that may be lying around. In the Light, we may see clearly where we are going – and we may guide others clearly also! Indeed, John probably has in mind a blend of the be<u>lie</u>ver not stumbling – and not causing others to stumble!

If my heart is really set on walking in the light; if my attitude is one that is really filled with a genuine desire to please Father God; then I myself will be saved from making many blunders, and I will be saved from causing others to make blunders! But if I am walking in darkness, then it means that I have not only lost the way myself, but that, in all probability, I have also led others into the darkness, and hurt others whom I have met in the dark.

George Duncan used to point out that some believers try to calculate how many they have helped, and led to a saving knowledge of the Lord Jesus. He would suggest that it might be a more beneficial – and humbling – exercise, and discipline, to think of the numbers we have hindered! I know that I am deeply challenged by that thought!

Christian assurance. How may I know that I am a disciple of Jesus? John gives these three tests – simple, yet profound.

Am I walking in the light?

Am I in union with the Lord Jesus, the Christ?

Am I obedient to the will of Father God?

If I am, then I may be assured, and can rejoice in that assurance – while constantly striving, in love, to become more and more like Jesus, co-operating with God the Holy Spirit in His work of sanctification in my life, trusting in Him day by day.

Do you have that assurance in your own heart? Praise God if you have – and then go and share your knowledge of Him with another. Have you no assurance? Then turn to Him, and seek the salvation that He so freely offers, even 'though it cost the blood of the only-begotten Son, and give Him all the glory and the praise.

Chapter 5

Growing in the Faith

In this chapter, and in the three verses that we are going to consider, we find John returning to the theme of the family of God.

> *"I am writing to you, little children, because your sins are forgiven for His sake. I am writing to you, fathers, because you know Him who is from the beginning. I am writing to you, young men, because you have overcome the evil one. I write to you, children, because you know the Father. I write to you, fathers, because you know Him Who is from the beginning. I write to you, young men, because you are strong, and the word of God abides in you, and you have overcome the evil one."* (vs.12-14).

These are three very lovely, and quite fascinating, verses. They are not, strictly speaking, poetry but, in the Greek language they have a strong rhythmical and poetical structure. The New English Bible is, in the English language, one version that brings that out (q.v.).

Academic theologians interpret these verses in two different ways and, indeed, either interpretation may be correct – there is not a vast difference between them, and what there is has to do with the grammatical structure! Rather than enter into a drawn-out discussion, I am taking the interpretation that seems to me to be more helpful!

Time and time again, in this letter, we have been led to think of the walk of the disciple of Jesus – i.e. the way and manner by which we live our lives. In the previous chapter, in particular, we thought on the progress in the life of the disciple that such a picture suggests. But progress may also be thought of in terms of growth, and this is what John is highlighting here. What he is doing is pointing to the varying stages of development at which the individual disciple may be found – stages which, of course, have to do not with physical age or stature, but with spiritual condition.

He points quite clearly to three stages that we may term as infancy. youth, and maturity – "*children*", "*young men*", and "*fathers*", to use John's own terms. Let's look at each in turn, beginning with the stage of spiritual infancy. And this, we find, concerns the pardon I have.

> "*I am writing to you, little children, because your sins are forgiven for His sake.*"

writes John. A little further on, for he makes a double, emphasising exhortation to each group, he writes:

> *"I write to you, children, because you know the Father."*

These are the earliest conscious experiences of the new-born child of God. Such a one rejoices in the forgiveness of his sins through the Christ, and in the consequent fellowship with God the Father. Sadly, this is as far as some ever go! Evangelical churches and mission halls are packed with spiritual babes – dear folk who love the Gospel, and that is about all that they do love; who know that the Gospel message is about the forgiveness of sins, but who know little or nothing else about it.

> *"little children"*

Let's note two things about the experience of these 'babes in Christ'. First of all, we consider what John finds in their experience.

And what he finds are these two tremendous truths that lie at the heart of every true conversion – the forgiveness we know we have from God, and the fellowship we find we have with God.

> *"… your sins are forgiven for His sake … … you know the Father."*

This is the central message of the Gospel, and we must not ever leave out the Cross, and its message of forgiveness.

"There's a way back to God from the dark paths of sin;
There's a door that is open, and you may go in.
At Calvary's cross is where you begin
When you come, as a sinner, to Jesus."

This was the message preached by the early church; this was the message that "turned the world upside down"; this was the message that won thousands, and tens of thousands into a living relationship with the Christ; this is the message that we must continue to preach at every opportunity. In the light of all that Jesus is; in the light of all that He has done; in the light of all that He has promised;

>*"your sins are forgiven"*,

and you may look into the face of your Creator, and call Him "Father" – even "Abba"!

But we must also note what John fears in their experience.

And this is something that is implied by the fact that he goes on to speak of further stages of spiritual growth. It is the fear of stagnation; of arrested growth and development.

The birth of a child, in the natural, physical, sense, is usually an occasion of great joy and celebration. We look at this little helpless bundle of humanity, and we go "Aw, isn't (s)he lovely?". We smile at the way in which that infant just lies there, looking all around, but understanding little, if anything. We watch as that child is fed by its mother, because it is totally unable to feed itself.

And all of that is perfectly normal! However, if we were to go on a long journey, and not return for several years. And if we were to visit that same family, and discover that same child – now seven or eight years old – still lying on its back, cooing and gurgling; still looking around but doing nothing; still being hand/breast-fed by its mother: then the earlier joy would be turned to deep sadness. Whatever hopes and dreams the parents may have had for their new-born child are not going to be realised.

How many become disciples of Jesus, but never seem to grow? Converted; born-again; knowing, and loving, the simple Gospel message; but that is all – and all of Father God's plans for their lives come to nothing! Of course, I am not referring to some who have specific mental/intellectual challenges, but to those who simply can't be bothered advancing in the faith.

When in my pastoral charge of Bellshill: St. Andrew's, I used to wonder if that was the problem there! I wondered if that was reason why we could have 150 attend the morning worship service, but only see one-third of that number in the evening. This wasn't simply that some of those who came in the morning did so out of no more than some sense of civic duty, or ecclesiastical obligation, while remaining unconverted; or that some were unable to attend because of family responsibilities; but that even some of those who were born-again had failed to grow, and were apparently not interested in growing!

The next stage to which John refers is youth. Here, his thinking centres around the power I need.

> *"I am writing to you, young men, because you have overcome the evil one. ... I write to you, young men, because you are strong, and the word of God abides in you, and you have overcome the evil one."*

So, the young men are those who are busily involved in the battle of Christian living. John Stott comments: "The Christian life, then, is not just enjoying the forgiveness and the fellowship of God, but fighting the enemy. The forgiveness of past sins must be followed by deliverance from sin's present power ..." Let's think of the activity of youth.

Youth is a turbulent time: there's so much to be done, and no-one else seems to be bothered! At least that was often the situation as perceived by the youth of my own day! That was when the phrase "angry young men" was popular – angry because of the state of the world, and the apathy of so many of its human inhabitants. I wonder what yesterday's "angry young men" think of today! Do we recognise any change? Have we now become the apathetic ones?

Life becomes more complicated in youth: temptations become more subtle, stronger; the forces to be vanquished are found to be more powerful than had been expected; ambition fills the mind. It's "go, go, go" – in one direction or another.

One clerical friend once described life as being rather like a ship that has been built and fitted out on the quiet waters of the Clyde – and that then has to sail into the full strength of the Atlantic gales. And that 'maiden voyage' corresponds to youth.

So it is with the disciple of Jesus – born-again of God the Holy Spirit. There comes a time when mere knowledge of forgiveness of sins through the shed blood of the Lord Jesus at Calvary becomes much more than that; when the voice is heard calling the Christian to battle. And, if we are truly growing in Jesus, then we respond!

I still recall, after so many decades, Sunday lunch in the home of my paternal grandmother – who lived next door to my parents and me. After the meal, this child of three to four years of age (me!) would stand up on an old arm-chair that was turned around (especially for the occasion?!) and use it as a "pulpit" while he led his "congregation" in the metrical version of the 23rd Psalm, to the well-known tune Crimond, followed by the disciples' prayer (aka "Our Father"!), before "dismissing" his little flock!

That was all well and good. However, it was much later when in my early twenties, I received a clear call to ministry that could not be ignored. It was that particular response that led me into the parish ministry in the Church of Scotland, and that involved me in academic study at University level; and in an area of service that I greatly enjoyed – until the Lord, in His wisdom, led me out of it. Of course, I was still involved in a preaching ministry (and continue to be!) and that always involves preparation and effort. It was necessary that I move on from childish things!

"Saved to serve" is now a very old Christian cliché, but one that must be constantly remembered by all of us who claim to be disciples of Jesus. If we are not to be stagnant believers, unmoving and lifeless, then we must go into battle for the Lord, serving Him with all that we have and are; every victory thrilling our souls; every achievement being a source of joy, and a challenge to further endeavour.

The activity of youth and, linked to it, the asking of youth.

Those of us who have, or have had, teenage children of our own are all too aware that youth is a time in which so much is asked for – money, clothes, freedom, sometimes even advice, and of course "Dad, may I borrow the car tonight?"

And it is, likewise, a time of asking in the spiritual life. As we mature in our faith, we see our own needs more clearly; we see the sufficiency of Jesus to meet those needs; and we ask – for joy; for peace; for power over sin, and power in service. And the wonderful thing is that, just as a loving human father delights in giving what is good, and helpful, and necessary, to his children, so the heavenly Father supplies all that His children need, out of His inexhaustible riches in Christ.

Spiritual youth: the period in which the disciple of Jesus is on active service. But before we leave this stage, let's note that the strength of the young men, by which they are able to

> "... *overcome the evil one* ..."

is not their own natural strength, for this would be sadly lacking. It's a conferred strength, even

> "... *the Word of God* ..."

that

> "... *abides in* ..."

them. Whether John is referring here to the Scriptures, as the written Word of God, or to the Divine Logos – the Word Who is Jesus, as the apostle explains in his account of the Gospel – is not clear. And it really doesn't matter! Indeed, it may well be that John intended the term to cover both.

Jesus' words, as John records them in Jn. 15:4 were

> "*Abide in Me, and I in you*";

while the Psalmist had asked the rhetorical question:

> "*How can a young man keep his way pure?*"

and answered it

> "*By guarding it, according to Your Word.*" (119:9)

which, he said

> "... *is a lamp to my feet, and a light to my path.*" (119:105).

And, of course, in Jesus the Word, the supreme revelation of the Father, we have the perfect example as we recall that He faced temptations greater than we can ever experience, in the wilderness – and repulsed the devil with the written Word, the

> "*sword of the Spirit*" (Eph.6:17)

that is

> "*sharper than any two-edged sword*" (Heb.4:12).

Spiritual infancy; spiritual youth; and the other stage in the life of the disciple of Jesus, to which John refers, is the stage of adulthood – spiritual maturity. Here John simply repeats himself:

> "*I am writing to you, fathers, because you know Him Who is from the beginning.*"

His emphasis in spiritual infancy was on the pardon I have; his emphasis in spiritual youth was on the power I need; and here, I would suggest, his emphasis is on the Person I know.

This, of course, is something different from the knowledge of the Father that we saw to be one of the marks of being a spiritual infant – of having started on the life of a disciple of Jesus. There, it is the knowledge of a new relationship; the assurance of the Father's love, experienced in fellowship. This knowledge, however, is of

> "... *Him Who is from the beginning.*"

John Stott comments: "All Christians, mature and immature, have come to know God. But their knowledge of Him ripens with the years. The little children know Him as "*the Father*"; the fathers have come to know Him as "*Him who is from the beginning*" which is probably a reference ... to the immutable, eternal God, Who does not change, as men change with advancing years, but Who is for ever the same." (*in loc*).

I've already mentioned the way in which my love for my wife has increased over the years – to the extent that the heart-bursting love that I had for her on the day on which we were married to one another is now seen as totally inadequate when set in the light of the deeper, more mature, love I have for her now. It's the same with my knowledge of her (and hers of me!). I thought that I knew her, all of those years ago. But, over those years, I have come to know her so much better – so much that we often find we are thinking the same thing, and will often start to say the same thing at the same time!

So then, this knowledge of the Father seems to take us into a much wider, and deeper, experience of the very nature and being of Almighty God.

Two brief comments may be made here, the first of which concerns the privilege of the intimacy that maturity enjoys.

There are many passages in the written Word to which we could make reference in this context. However, my favourite example is one that Rev George B. Duncan frequently used. It's found in Ps.103:7 where it is recorded about the great leader of the Children of Israel, Moses, that Almighty God

> "... *made known His ways to Moses; His acts to the people of Israel.*"

That is to say, Father God let Moses, His mature servant, into the inner workings of His mind; the people, whose faith – where it existed – was so immature, simply saw the result of His actions. Maturity, in the physical realm, brings with it a certain intimacy that we may rightly count as a privilege. It is no less so in the realm of the spirit. But there are also pressures – the pressures of the responsibilities that maturity receives.

As we get older (less young!); as our position in the family, or in our job, rises; we are landed with ever-increasing responsibility, and all of the additional pressures that it brings with it. Growing maturity leads to growing responsibility – even if only due to the fact that more is expected from us!

If we are in this stage of spiritual development, we will also be carrying more and more of the burdens of responsibility

– in the realm of our prayer-life; in the matter, and measure, of our financial giving; in the manner, and form, of our Christian service. And this responsibility will be gladly accepted; cheerfully borne; willingly fulfilled; and faithfully, and diligently, carried through.

Three stages of spiritual growth – infancy, youth, and maturity – each with its own particular emphasis. And, since spiritual growth has no co-relation to physical growth, the obvious question is "Where do you, where do I, stand right now?"

Yet there is a very real sense in which each of these emphases can exist simultaneously; a sense in which, no matter how mature any of us may be in our spiritual life, there is still something of both the child, and the youth, in us. For we always need to be reminded of the pardon we have; and we are constantly in need of the power of God in our lives. God grant that each one of us may know Him in such a way that real spiritual maturity may be seen in us; that we may be fed, not just with milk, but with the solid food of the Word, continuing to

> "... *grow in the grace and knowledge of our Lord and Saviour Jesus Christ. To him be the glory both now and to the day of eternity.*" (II Peter 3:18).

Chapter 6.

Developing as a disciple of Jesus.

In the previous chapter, we examined the light, shed by John, on different stages of spiritual development in the life of the disciple of Jesus. However, John is constantly aware of the potential for his words to be taken wrongly. Those words, he realised, might well have led to certain complacency on part of some: "Don't expect too much from me; I'm only a child in the faith"! So, in this next brief section of his letter, he pinpoints the hindrances to development, as he looks at the relationship of the disciple of Jesus to the world.

> *"Do not love the world or the things in the world. If anyone loves the world, love for the Father is not in him. For all that is in the world, the lust of the flesh and the lust of the eyes and the pride of life, is not of the Father but is of the world. And the world passes away, and the lust of it; but he who does the will of God abides for ever."* (2:15-17)

It is clear that John is conscious of the fact that what he refers to as "*the world*" constitutes an element of real danger, and that fact is highlighted not only here, but also in other parts of the letter, and in his record of the Gospel. Consider three aspects of *"the world"*, first of which concerns the discernment the disciple of Jesus will require.

It's a discernment as to what is **meant** by *"the world"* that John says we are not to love.

> *"Do not love the world or the things in the world."*

Two comments need to be made here, first of which concerns the way in which *"the world"* can be defined.

Obviously, John isn't referring to the people in the world. We are told, in Jn.3:16 that

> *"… God so loved the world that He gave His only Son, that whoever believes in Him should not perish but have eternal life."*

If God loved, and loves, the world in this sense – i.e. the people of the world whom He created – then it would be wrong for us not to love them! Indeed, we read that

> *"… one of the scribes came up and heard* [Jesus and the Pharisees] *disputing with one another, and seeing that He answered them well, asked Him, "Which commandment is the first of all?" Jesus answered, "The first is, 'Hear, O Israel: The Lord our God, the Lord is one; and you shall love the Lord your God with all your heart, and with all your soul, and with all your mind, and with all your strength.' The second is this, 'You shall love your neighbour as yourself.'*

> *There is no other commandment greater than these."*
> (Mark 12:28-31).

Obviously, John is not referring, here, to people.

Nor is he referring to world of nature, which is the creation of God. Again, and again, Jesus takes His parables, and illustrations, from world of nature and its processes: Sower and seed; wheat and tares; vineyard; sheep and goats; etc. Surely we can love the world of nature, and enjoy the beauty of the countryside; the singing of the birds; the glory of a sunset over the Western Isles.

What, then, does John mean by this term, "*the world*"? He means that part of the life of mankind that is totally incompatible with the mind and character of God. It is what we have already noted is, in the words of C.H.Dodd: "… human society insofar as it is organised on wrong principles, and characterised by base desires," Prof Barclay – who speaks more readily to the non-academic! – writes that "… to John, the world was nothing other than pagan society with its false values, and its false standards, and its false gods. The world, in this passage," he continues, "does not mean the world in general, for God so loved the world which He had made; it means the world which, in fact, had forsaken the God Who made it."

"*the world*", then, is those base desires, false values, and egoism; that moral order; that way of life; that scale of values; those customs, pursuits, interests; that are not in harmony with the mind and will of Almighty God. This is not simply "anti-God", but "a-God"; not just rejecting God, but neglecting Him!

The second comment concerns the way in which "*the world*" is described. John describes it by setting out three sins that are typical sins of "*the world*":

> "*the lust of the flesh, and the lust of the eyes, and the pride of life.*"

or, as J.B.Phillips translates it:

> "*men's primitive desires; their greedy ambitions; and the glamour of all that they think splendid*".

Here are what, as we've already noted, C.H.Dodd refers to as "base desires, false values, and egoism." "*The world*" is concerned with self-gratification; with superficial values; with self-importance. And worldliness is the self-centred and self-pleasing pattern of life, so common in our contemporary culture. It is, quite simply, putting self first – and God, if He gets a place at all, a very poor second.

What a contrast to another John – the Baptiser – who said of the Lord Jesus, as John records in his account of the Gospel:

> "*He must increase, but I must decrease.*" (3:30).

How different from the teaching of Jesus, Himself:

> "*If any man would come after Me, let him deny himself and take up his cross and follow Me.*" (Matt. 16:24).

If the disciple of Jesus is to grow, and mature, there is a discernment that he/she will require. But there is also a defilement that such a disciple must avoid.

John states, very clearly, that

> "... *all that is in the world, ...*";

all the things that he has just mentioned –

> "... *the lust of the flesh and the lust of the eyes and the pride of life, ...*";

all of these things are

> "... *not of the Father.*"

Worldliness had no place at all in the mind and life of Father God; and should, therefore, have no place in the minds and lives of His children! John would appear to have, in the back of **his** mind, the task of the disciple of Jesus in the world.

Later on, he will state quite explicitly that

> "*as [Jesus] is, so are we in this world*" (4:17).

In other words, if we are truly disciples of Jesus; born again of God the Holy Spirit; our task in the world is to be as Jesus' task! And, since He came into the world in order to redeem mankind, and to reveal the fullness of the character of Father God, so the task of the disciple is to proclaim that redemptive plan and purpose of God, and to reveal God to man!

One of the most amazing statements ever made by Paul, the apostle to the Gentiles, was

> "*Christ ... lives in me*" (Gal.2:20).

And, akin to that is his affirmation that

> "... *to me, to live, is Christ.*" (Phil.1:21).

Now, if Christ lives in me; if He is life itself to me; then I should reveal Him to others – and in doing so, draw others to Him! And this task is not some optional extra for the few who don a clerical collar, or who go to the foreign mission-field. This is a total obligation on the whole of the Body of the Christ – to proclaim the Good News of the redeeming love of Almighty God, the Creator and Sustainer of all that exists; and to reveal Him to a needy world of men and women, boys and girls.

I am constantly reminded, and remind others, that the words of the risen, soon to be ascended, Lord Jesus to His disciples were:

> "... *you shall receive power when the Holy Spirit has come upon you; and you shall be **my witnesses** in Jerusalem and in all Judea and Samaria and to the end of the earth.*" (Acts 1:8; *emphasis added*).

Two things may be noted. First of all that He used the word "witnesses", not "evangelists". The latter is one of the gifts of the Lord Jesus

> "... *to equip the saints for the work of ministry, for building up the body of Christ, ...*" (Eph.4:12).

The former – witnesses – is what every disciple is called to be. The only question is: "Am I a good witness to the Lord Jesus – or a poor one?"!

But, closely linked with this thought of the task of the believer in the world, there is the thought of the threat to the believer in the world. And that threat is, quite simply, that the world will spoil the testimony and witness of the disciple of Jesus. How can a worldly Christian, whose life is cluttered up with ideas, pursuits, and standards, which have nothing at all in common with the mind of God the Father, even begin to represent Him? What sort of a picture of God does that kind of "Christian" present to the world?

Some may have heard the old poem:

"Christ has no hands but our hands to do His work today;
He has no feet but our feet to lead men in His way.
He has no tongue but our tongues to tell men how He died;
He has no help but our help to bring them to His side.

We are the only Bible the careless world will read;
We are the sinner's Gospel; we are the scoffer's creed.
We are the Lord's last message given in deed and word;
What if the type is crooked? What if the print is blurred?"

We might add the question: "What if the glass is cracked, and the frame dirty, in which a beautiful painting is displayed?" Surely the painting isn't seen to its best advantage – if it can be noticed at all!

The kind of Christians whose way of life, whose attitudes, whose standards, whose pursuits, are identical with those of the world are, at best, showing forth Jesus in a very bad light and, at worst, deceiving themselves in thinking that they are disciples of Jesus in the first place!

James speaks of the need of the disciple of Jesus to keep himself

>"... *from being polluted by the world.*" (1:27; NIV),

while Peter refers to the disciple as someone who has escaped from

>"... *the corruption that is in the world.*" (II Pet 1:4).

A worldly, or 'carnal' Christian is a negation of the Gospel; a contradiction of the truth of God; a parody of the way of life to which the disciple of Jesus is called. It is just as if the son of the owner of a laundry went about in filthy clothes – he is not much of an advertisement for his father's business!

This, then, is the defilement that the disciple of Jesus must avoid – defilement by worldly living.

A discernment that will be required; a defilement that must be avoided; and, in addition, there is a detachment the disciple of Jesus must maintain.

Let's think here of the environment in which the disciple of Jesus will be found. Whilst the believer is told not to love the worldliness of the world, John is as well aware as anyone that the disciple of Jesus must live in the world! Jesus, Himself, prayed in the Garden of Gethsemane:

>"*My prayer is not that You take them out of the world but that You protect them from the evil one.*" (John 17:15; NIV).

This, of course, is part of the paradox of living as a disciple of Jesus – being in the world, but not of the world! Those of my own generation may remember the words sung by Jim Reeves:

"This world is not my home; I'm just a passin' through.
My treasures are laid up somewhere beyond the blue.
The angels beckon me from heaven's open door;
and I can't feel at home in this world anymore."

Someone has said that "The Christian is not ruined be living in the world, but by the world living in him."! I read, somewhere, that flies that gather at a river will plunge their bodies into the water – but keep their wings dry! You and I, in the world, need to keep our wings of faith and love dry!

The disciple of Jesus is not meant to be withdrawn from the world i.e. he is not to be removed, as were/are some of the monastic orders, from physical contact with people who are ungodly and unconverted. But although he will have physical contact with them, at a social level, he has little in common with their way of life; their standards of living. Back to the flies. On a hot day, in the garden, it is well-nigh impossible to avoid them – but I don't have to be one of them!

As I was sharing on this letter from John with the group of anglophones, here in France, we had a discussion one morning, on 'Christian fellowship'. One of them sent out an e-mail sharing some further thoughts he had had on the subject. In it he wrote: "Should we then show two fingers to those who are not in fellowship with Christ and His saints?

God forbid! I have grandchildren, children, whom I love deeply; I have friends whose friendship spans over 60 years. We have shared companionship and friendship and still do, but I cannot share the fellowship of Christ with them. I long for a time when we can, but until that day dawns, and it will, I shall continue to pray for them and, of course, be their companion still."

The disciple of Jesus is in the world for the purposes of God. We are in this environment is order to exercise the responsibility that Father God has laid upon us.

Of course, we must be careful not to allow the pendulum swing too far in the other direction! So what I have just said should not be taken as an encouragement to go everywhere where the unconverted go – even if the intention is their salvation! God the Holy Spirit doesn't operate in that way at all, and other opportunities, in more conducive surroundings, will be found – if only we keep ourselves open to the Spirit's promptings.

The environment in which the disciple of Jesus will be found is the world – that physical environment that we all have in common. But the threat to the believer needs to be emphasised yet again, and so we must note the enslavement from which the disciple of Jesus must be free.

"Do not love the world …" (v.15).

Never allow the world to capture your loyalty, or your love; never allow the values, that are purely worldly values, i.e. the product of unconverted thinking, never allow these values to shape your life. However, that is not easy! We are susceptible to pressure from advertisers; from our peer group; from our natural family. But John is quite clear:

> "*Do not love the world ...*"

There is nothing as dominating as love; nothing as compelling; as constraining; as controlling. The ways of the world can be made to appear very attractive – the devil sees to that! But nothing that the world has to offer can last.

At Keswick, all those years ago, Eric Alexander pointed out that the transience of the world is a theme that runs through the whole of the written Word of God, and he reminded us of the words of the hymn:

"Fading, is the worldling's pleasure;
All his boasted pomp and show.
Solid joys and lasting treasure
None but Zion's children know."

There is nothing durable in what the world has to offer.

The world, then, is something from which the disciple of Jesus must be different. There are times when we must "stick out like a sore thumb"! Inwardly we must be different in our attitudes; outwardly, we must be different in our actions. And, of course, it is this very difference that the world resents! "Conform!", it demands. But God's Word says, all too plainly for some:

> "*Do not be conformed to this world but be transformed by the renewal of your mind, ...*" (Rom 12:2).

The disciple who has the courage of his/her convictions shows the worldling - and, sometimes, even other believers! – for what he is, and that is why such a disciple can be very unpopular in certain circles! But the true disciple of Jesus must be free from the enslavement of social opinion; of the fear of man. He must be free from these enslavements in order that he may be free for the doing of the will of God for his life; free to serve God in the way to which He has called; free to live a life that will commend God to others.

In the broadest sense, there are only two belief systems: theism and naturalism. One believes in supernatural influence on the affairs of men and as the foundation of purpose and order, the other does not. The vast majority of the world is theistic (though not creationist) in its worldview. Only the "civilised world" is arrogant enough to consciously exclude the supernatural from its thinking. But this is the key:

> "*For as he thinketh in his heart, so is he*" (Proverbs 23:7).

This is why we are clearly told,

> "*Keep thy heart with all diligence, for out of it are the issues of life*" (Proverbs 4:23).

Underlying all, of course, is the great Adversary, who seeks to draw the worship of all men to himself and replace all "gods" as the god of this world. Satan is driven, like

> "*… a roaring lion,*"

to devour all who oppose him (1 Peter 5:8). The real war is a spiritual one (see Ephesians 6:12-13). President George W. Bush was correct when he insisted that the campaign against modern terrorism will be "unlike any other we have ever seen." It will be worldwide in scope, transcultural in impact, and years in the execution.

Will terrorists be eliminated and evil conquered? Not until Jesus Christ sets up His millennial reign. But we can

>"*overcome evil with good*" (Romans 12:21),

and we can

>"*reign in life*" (Romans 5:17).

Freedom is administered through truth (John 8:32, 36), and Satan, when resisted in

>"*the faith*" (1 Peter 5:9),

will

>"*flee*" (James 4:7).

>"*Who is sufficient for these things?*"

asked Paul, in a not altogether different context (II Cor 2:16). The answer, sadly, is "No-one" – at least no-one in their own strength! That's why we depend on, and rejoice in, the strength that is available to us through the indwelling of God the Holy Spirit. That's why there is a discernment the disciple of Jesus will require; a defilement the disciple of Jesus must avoid; and a detachment the disciple of Jesus must maintain.

May we may indeed live as is pleasing to Him; excelling and thinking on

> "... *whatever is true, whatever is honourable, whatever is just, whatever is pure, whatever is lovely, whatever is gracious,*"

whatever is

> "*worthy of praise.*" (Phil 4:8).

And we will be careful to give to Him, all of the glory, all of the honour, and all of the praise.

Chapter 7.

Family characteristics.

Annually, at the time of Rosh Hashanah (the Jewish New Year) there is a time of self-examination leading up to Yom Kippur – the Day of Atonement. It's a special time in which devout Jews request forgiveness from those they have wronged and extend forgiveness to those who have wronged them. Jewish tradition, in fact, holds that God cannot forgive us for sins that we commit against another until we obtain forgiveness from the person we wronged. Was this in the mind of the Saviour when He provided us with, not a set of words to be repeated, parrot-fashion, every Sunday, but a model prayer – a blue print – with the familiar words:

"Forgive us our sins …?

Forgiveness and saying "Sorry" can be life changing. Both are crucial to leaving the past behind, and moving forward with God's plan for our lives. Asking for forgiveness is pivotal to repentance, a closer walk with God, and to successful relationships with our family, friends and our fellowman.

In the previous chapter, covering vs 15-17 of this 2nd chap of John's first letter, we looked at the danger to the disciple of Jesus that John saw as coming from "*the world*". And we found that "*the world*" could be defined as "… human society insofar as it is organised on wrong principles, and characterised by base desires, false values, and egoism." (C.H.Dodd); or, more simply, "… nothing other than pagan society with its false values, and its false standards, and its false gods. … the world which, in fact, had forsaken the God Who made it." (W.Barclay). So what John was concerned about was the behaviour of those who claimed to be disciples of Jesus, and he pointed out the need for the believer, while living in the physical and Godless world, not to be defiled by it, but rather to witness to it.

But effective witnessing requires an informed faith – one must be accurate in what one presents as the Gospel of the Lord Jesus, the Christ. So John turns now to another danger – this time not to do with the behaviour of the disciple of Jesus, but with the beliefs that are held by those who call themselves "Christians".

The words at which we look are found at the end of the second chapter:

"Children, it is the last hour; and as you have heard that antichrist is coming, so now many antichrists have come; therefore we know that it is the last hour. They went out from us, but they were not of us; for if they had been of us, they

would have continued with us; but they went out, that it might be plain that they all are not of us. But you have been anointed by the Holy One, and you all know. I write to you, not because you do not know the truth, but because you know it, and know that no lie is of the truth. Who is the liar but he who denies that Jesus is the Christ? This is the antichrist, he who denies the Father and the Son. No one who denies the Son has the Father. He who confesses the Son has the Father also. Let what you heard from the beginning abide in you. If what you heard from the beginning abides in you, then you will abide in the Son and in the Father. And this is what he has promised us, eternal life.

I write this to you about those who would deceive you; but the anointing which you received from Him abides in you, and you have no need that any one should teach you; as His anointing teaches you about everything, and is true, and is no lie, just as it has taught you, abide in Him.

And now, little children, abide in Him, so that when He appears we may have confidence and not shrink from Him in shame at His coming. If you know that He is righteous, you may be sure that every one who does right is born of Him."

By way of introduction, we may note that there is a certain mentality that under-rates belief. There are those who will claim that it doesn't matter what you believe as long as you are sincere! But the truth of the matter is that the more sincere you are, the more important it is that what you believe is true! There isn't much point in being sincerely – wrong!

Or there are those who completely divorce belief and behaviour by saying that it is the latter that is important – it doesn't matter what you believe just as long as you are a "nice" person! What they forget is that what a person believes dictates, to a great extent, their behaviour! People have, in the past and under the influence of hallucinogenic drugs, jumped off tower blocks – in the belief that they could fly! That was dangerous and, in some cases, sadly, fatal! Even as you sit, quietly reading this book, you are doing so because you believe that the house in which you are reading (if, indeed, you are reading in your home – the principle applies to any other building) is solidly built on sound foundations. But if you believed that the house was on fire, and about to come crashing down around you, then I would suggest that you would behave in a very different manner!

In v.26 John writes:

> "*I write this to you about those who would deceive you;*"

There were forces at work that were out to damage the life of the church, and their attack was centred upon the beliefs

– the doctrines, if you will – of the disciples. John was concerned that these people might be recognised, and that the corruption they taught might be evaded.

So, in order that his aim might be fulfilled, we find that he describes them.

> *"Children, it is the last hour; and as you have heard that antichrist is coming, so now many antichrists have come; therefore we know that it is the last hour."*

Prof Barclay has written no less than seven full pages, in his Daily Study Bible, on this one verse! I do not intend to write as much! However, we must deal with two points that call for some clarification.

First of these concerns the phrase "the last hour". What does John mean by these words? Is he using the expression to describe the whole Christian era; or is he saying – mistakenly – that it is the last hour before the Lord Jesus raptures His true saints; or is he using the phrase to describe a particular situation? The latter would appear to be the case. He is, in fact, expressing a theological truth, rather than providing a chronological sequence/reference. Even the word translated "hour" may be used, figuratively, to describe a "season". As he looked at this, still fledgling, church he could see that the powers of darkness were closing their ranks; that the forces of evil were rallying.

May I suggest that what we are dealing with, here, is the relationship between time and eternity[4]?! Contrary to popular belief – sometimes reinforced by the words of otherwise great songs – eternity is not "endless time", but "timelessness." There is a kind of anthropomorphism in John's words. He is writing to those who live in what is referred to as "the time-space continuum" – in other words, we are confined to the spatial dimensions of length, breadth, and height/depth, and of time. Those of us who have a saving, vital, relationship with Father God, through the atoning sacrifice of the Son, and the indwelling of Holy Spirit, are also acutely aware of the spiritual dimension (as, indeed, are many who relate to different spirits), but there may be other dimensions that are beyond our human knowledge and the comprehension of our mortal minds.

So, in a very real sense, it is always "the last hour" for the disciple of Jesus. The Son, in His humanity, did not know the day or the hour of His return – and we certainly do not know. But we must live our lives as if it is just about to happen! "That Antichrist would come [John] and his readers knew, and in the false teachers he discerned the agents or, at least, the forerunners of Antichrist, sharing his nature so completely that they could be called 'many antichrists'." (F.F.Bruce, *op cit*; p.65).

---

[4] This is another of the "Great Words of the Faith" dealt with in my first book.

John Stott comments: "What John wrote was true. And it is still true. The fact that that more than 1900 years have elapsed since he wrote ... does not invalidate ... or contradict his affirmation. It is still 'the last hour'; the hour of final opposition to Christ."

The characteristics of the time have not changed. Indeed, they have intensified. So we have, today, even those who wear clerical garb (and I retain a full set of pulpit robes and accoutrements in a suitcase in my study, and have no problem with that mode of dress, *per se*!) who will proclaim, for example, that Jesus is not the only way to the Father. And this in spite of His own clear, and unequivocal, statement:

> "*I am the Way, and the Truth, and the Life; no one comes to the Father, **but by Me**.*" (John 14:6).

These were, and continue to be, the false teachers of whom Jesus, Himself, warned (see Mk.13:22) and who were causing so much trouble to those for whom John had pastoral responsibility. Is it making too big a claim to suggest that the church in these early years of the 21st century has many "antichrists" in its midst – those who make a profession that they are "Christians" (one reason why I now prefer to use the expression "disciples of Jesus"!), but who happily endorse abortion; the remarriage of divorcees, and the leadership positions of such; the so-called "marriage" of homosexuals and lesbians; the distortion, and dilution, of the Gospel message; and other anti-Biblical teaching? Is this state of affairs a constant reminder to us that, as John Stott has stated, it is still, "*the last hour*"?

Which leads us on, nicely, to the second point. There is an implicit reference to these deceivers as those who are in opposition to the Christ. But John is also totally explicit as he refers to them as "*antichrists*". This term defines their teaching, as he explains in vs.22-23:

> "*Who is the liar but he who denies that Jesus is the Christ? This is the antichrist, he who denies the Father and the Son. No one who denies the Son has the Father. He who confesses the Son has the Father also.*"

These people were not only opposed to the Christ; they also denied His deity! And even in the established churches, there are those, today, who do the same thing!

Turning, again, to John Stott – whose compact commentary on this letter is very helpful – he writes: "The heretics' theology is not just defective; it is diabolical! The fundamental doctrinal test of the professing Christian concerns his view of the Person of Jesus. If he is a Unitarian, or a member of a sect denying the deity of Jesus, **he is not a Christian**. Many strange cults," he continues, "which have a popular appeal today [early 60s], can be easily judged, and quickly repudiated, by this test." (*emphasis added*).

> "*What do you think about the Christ?*" (Matt.22:42).

Jesus Himself once asked some of the Pharisees. It is a question that must still be asked if we are to evade, and avoid, the spiritual corruption that abounds today!

But having described these deceivers, John goes on to disown them.

> "... *they went out from us,*"

he writes,

> "***but they were not of us*** ..."! (*my emphasis*)

In other words, they made a profession of faith; they claimed to be disciples of Jesus; but they were making a false profession! A friend with whom I shared in the leadership team of what was then the largest charismatic fellowship in Scotland, used to say – "You cannot be in the Kingdom of God without being in membership of the church; but you can be in membership in the church without being in the Kingdom of God!" In other words, it is all too easy to be a member of a congregation; to have your name on the congregational roll/register; to be a leading member within a denomination; yet not really belong to Jesus! These heretics may have been nominal members, with their names "on the roll"; but they were not a part of the living body of the living Christ!

There are, sadly, those who share our earthly company, but not our heavenly birth. Now, only the Lord Himself knows for certain those who are His (II Tim.2:19); only on the final Day of separation will the wheat and the tares be completely revealed; but, in the meantime, some are made manifest in their true colours by their beliefs, and by their behaviour.

These people couldn't stay in the fellowship, because they were not of it.

> "... *if they had been of us,*"

writes John,

> "*they would have continued with us ...*"

and continuing is a test and a sign of genuineness. That's something we recognise in our prayer-life. If you ask me to pray for you concerning some specific situation, I will readily agree to do so. But if I pray for only a couple of days, or even a couple of weeks, while the matter is still not resolved, I have shown that my concern for you was less genuine than it may have, at first, appeared to be! It's when I continue to pray, month after month; maybe year after year; that I show that I am genuine. The departure of these men showed their real spiritual condition. There was, and is, corruption in the church that the true disciple of Jesus must evade.

But John is a wise old teacher. He knows that negative teaching, alone, doesn't always help. And so he speaks a positive word as well, as he thinks on the communion the disciple of Jesus should enjoy.

He refers to this in v.20 and, again, in v.27 where he speaks of an "*anointing*" that the followers of the Christ have all received.

> "... *you have been anointed by the Holy One, and you all know.*"
>
> "... *the anointing which you received from Him abides in you, ...*"

The anointing they have received is the anointing of God the Holy Spirit. And it is His presence, and power, and ministry; it is communion with Him; that is the safeguard against error in doctrine. This was the promise of Jesus that

> "... *when He, the Spirit of truth shall come, He shall guide you into all truth.*" (Jn 16:13),

a promise many often claim before turning to God's Word!

But John also lays stress on the little word "*all*" –

> "... *you all know ...*"

These people who were attacking the Christian faith claimed to have 'special knowledge'; they claimed a kind of 'spiritual one-upmanship'; they were, you may recall, of the school of thought that we refer to as Gnosticism. So John emphasises that all have knowledge; that spiritual knowledge and insight are not the prerogative of a privileged few, but the right and experience of every true disciple of Jesus.

"There are, of course, matters of technical scholarship, of language, of history, of technical theology, that must be the preserve of the expert; but the essentials of the faith are the possession of every man." (William Barclay).

Indeed, it is one of the wonders of the Christian faith that, while it is so profound that the greatest intellect could spend a lifetime studying it, and never do more than scratch the surface, yet all that is required to be known for salvation, is able to be understood by even a child.

And John emphasises that he is not bringing his readers any new message in what he writes:

> "*I write to you, not because you do not know the truth, but because you know it, …*" (v.21).

In other words, he is simply reminding, and exhorting, that what is already known become active, effective, and operative in our lives. George Duncan would often say that most preaching is like this – not the bringing of a completely new message, but the reminding of what is already known, and the urging that it be acted upon.

James reminds us that we should

> "… *be doers of the word, and not hearers only, deceiving yourselves. For if anyone is a hearer of the word and not a doer, he is like a man who observes his natural face in a mirror; for he observes himself and goes away and at once forgets what he was like. But he who looks into the perfect law, the law of liberty, and perseveres, being no hearer that forgets but a doer that acts, he shall be blessed in his doing.*" (James 1:22-25).

Prof. Barclay comments: "It is the simple fact of the Christian life that life would be different at once if we would only put into practice that which we already know. That is not to say that we never need to learn anything new; but it is to say that, even as we are, we have light enough to walk by, if we use the light we have."

But even as John thinks of this communion that disciples of Jesus should enjoy in the teaching ministry, and the anointing of God the Holy Spirit, he also recalls that aspect of "continuing" to which he has already made reference. And so, he reminds his flock, there is an abiding they must secure.

> *"Let what you heard from the beginning abide in you"*, he writes. *"If what you heard from the beginning abides in you, then you will abide in the Son and in the Father ... the anointing which you have received from Him abides in you ..."*

and a repeated exhortation to

> *"... abide in Him."*

What they had heard, of course, was the Gospel. And here we have another part of the safeguard – the Spirit of God linked to the Word of God.

How important it is to have a Holy Spirit-guided knowledge of the written Word. It is the lack of such knowledge – which is much more than the head-knowledge that one may obtain by going to Bible College or University – that makes so many easy prey for the exponents of the modern cults and heresies: Mormons; Jehovah's Witnesses; Christian Scientists; to name just some of the better-known.

It was with the written Word of God, as contained in the Tanakh (what we know as the Old Testament) that Jesus vanquished the devil in the wilderness; and it is with that same Word, the

> *"sword of the Spirit ... sharper than any two-edged sword"* (Heb.4:12)

that we may defeat the devil today.

There is, then, a corruption that the disciple of Jesus must evade. And this is done by entering into a communion that the disciple of Jesus should enjoy. And so will come the conclusion the disciple of Jesus will expect.

John speaks of the coming that should delight the child of God.

> *"And now, little children, abide in Him so that, when He appears, we may have confidence, and not shrink from Him in shame at His coming."*

A disciple of Jesus, whose belief and behaviour have been maintained in such a way as to be pleasing to Father God, will look forward to the rapture of the saints with a great longing and desire.

The whole doctrine of the Second Coming – which, I would contend is in two parts – is still a neglected doctrine in much of the main stream of the Christian church. Of course, there are those who make predictions that even the Son said He could not make. But they tend to be looked upon as the kind of lunatic fringe that, in spite of the undoubted sincerity of some, they really are!

Yet the New Testament makes clear that Jesus **will** return.

> *"So when they had come together, they asked Him, 'Lord, will You at this time restore the kingdom to Israel?' He said to them, 'It is not for you to know times or seasons which the Father has fixed by His own authority. But you shall receive power when the Holy Spirit has come upon you; and you shall be My witnesses in Jerusalem and in all Judea and Samaria and to the end of the earth. And when He had said this, as they were looking on, He was lifted up, and a cloud took Him out of their sight. And while they were gazing into heaven as He went, behold, two men stood by them in white robes, and said, 'Men of Galilee, why do you stand looking into heaven? This Jesus, Who was taken up from you into heaven, will come in the same way as you saw Him go into heaven'."* (Acts 1:6-11).

"The one Who came as Bethlehem's Babe will be the same One Who will return as conquering Judge. The same truth that He brought at His first coming will be the basis of judgment at the second. Those who remain in Him may, therefore, live without fear or shame in anticipation of that final event." (Asbury Bible Commentary; *in loc.*)

Do you believe that the Lord Jesus shall return in power and glory? What does such a thought do to you? Some, it must fill with dread; it's the last thing they would want to happen! But if we are truly children of God, and not just members of a congregation, nominal church-goers, then we will delight in the prospect; look for it; long for it.

"Christ is coming! Let creation
From her groans and travail cease;
Let the glorious proclamation
Hope restore, and faith increase.
Christ is coming! Christ is coming!
Come, Thou blessed Prince of Peace"

Can you sing words such as those with all of your heart, and souls, and mind? Or what about the words from another of the older hymns

"… O come quickly
Alleluia! Come, Lord, come."?

Would you mean that invitation? The coming of the Lord Jesus, the Christ – Yeshua HaMashiach – should delight the child of God.

Finally, in this section, John refers to the conduct that should befit the child of God.

He speaks of the possibility of being shamed away from Jesus, at His coming.

> *"And now, little children, abide in Him, so that when He appears we may have confidence and not shrink from Him in shame at His coming."*

He also reminds us of the necessity of right doing as evidence that we are truly born of the Spirit of God.

> "*If you know that He is righteous, you may be sure that every one who does right is born of Him.*"

As the child of my parents, I should be exhibiting something of their character; their nature. And if I were to fail to do so, then even although both are dead, I should be ashamed. As those who claim to be children of God – not simply because He is ultimately responsible for our existence, but in a deep, relational sense – we should be exhibiting something of His character and nature, lest we

> "*… shrink from Him in shame at His coming.*",

just like a child who has been misbehaving during its parents' absence, is ashamed to come into their presence on their return.

What a tragedy if we who, compared with so many of even our fellow disciples of Jesus, are so richly blessed, should be like that! We are meant to live, every day, in a way that is worthy of Him Whose Name we bear, lest we are shamed away from His presence at His coming.

Of course, the secret is bound up in those three words to which we have already referred:

> "*Abide in Him*".

The great need, today, is not for more nominal "church members" – God Himself knows that we have enough of them and to spare. The need is for Spirit-filled, and Bible-centred, disciples of Jesus who do, indeed, *"abide in Him"*, and who thus

> *"… may have confidence and not shrink from Him in shame at His coming."*

Chapter 8.

Being "in the family"

After a longer section in the previous chapter, we now turn to just three verses at the beginning of what we know as chapter 3. Remember, of course, that John did not write his letter in chapters and verses any more than would you or I – these are much later additions for the convenience of finding any particular passage. The chapter divisions commonly used today were developed by Stephen Langton, an Archbishop of Canterbury. Langton put the modern chapter divisions into place in around A.D. 1227. The Wycliffe English Bible of 1382 was the first Bible to use this chapter pattern. Since the Wycliffe Bible, nearly all Bible translations have followed Langton's chapter divisions.

The Hebrew Tanakh (the "Old Testament") was divided into verses by a Jewish rabbi by the name of Nathan in A.D. 1448. Robert Estienne – a Parisian – who was also known by the Latin name of Stephanus, was the first to divide the New Testament into standard numbered verses, in 1555.

Stephanus essentially used Nathan's verse divisions for the Old Testament. Since that time, beginning with the Geneva Bible, the chapter and verse divisions employed by Stephanus have been accepted into nearly all the Bible versions.

> *"See what love the Father has given us, that we should be called children of God; and so we are. The reason why the world does not know us is that it did not know Him. Beloved, we are God's children now; it does not yet appear what we shall be, but we know that when He appears we shall be like Him, for we shall see Him as He is. And every one who thus hopes in Him purifies himself as He is pure."*

We have, in these few verses, a veritable outburst of wonder and excitement at the vista of the love of Almighty God. The Greek word translated, in the AV(KJV)

> *"… what manner of …"* (ποταπην – *potapen*)

always implies astonishment. We might legitimately expand those words to read:

> *"Behold, what astoundingly, amazingly, out-of-this-world, kind of love the Father has given us, …"*

And this eulogy; this paean of praise and adoration; this exhilarating enthusiasm; is brought about by the mention, in the last verse of the previous chapter, of being

> *"… born of Him."*

John sees this new birth as being, as it were, a guarantee of God's love for, and interest in, each one of us.

> *"Consider the incredible love that the Father has shown to us in allowing us to be called 'children of God'..."*

is how J.B.Phillips translates the beginning of v.1.

But permit me to emphasise, as I have done before, and without any apology for doing so again, that the expression *"children of God"* only applies to those who have come to Him, in repentance and faith, and committed themselves to Jesus the Christ. It applies only to those who are truly members of the church – the Body, and the Bride, of the Christ – and not merely members of some denominational institution.

William Barclay comments, in his inimitably clear manner: "There is something here which we may well note. **It is by the gift of God that a man becomes a child of God.** By nature, man is the creature of God, because God is His Creator; but is by grace that man becomes the child of God." He continues: "There are two English (language) words which are closely connected, but whose meanings are widely different. There is the word 'paternity', and the word 'fatherhood'. 'Paternity' describes a relationship in which a father is responsible for the physical existence of a son; but, as far as paternity goes, it can be, and it not infrequently happens, that the father has never even set eyes on the son, and would not recognise him if, in later years he met him.

'Fatherhood' describes an intimate, loving, continuous, relationship in which father and son grow closer to each other every day. In the sense of 'paternity'," the professor concludes, "all men are children of God; but in the sense of 'fatherhood', men are only children of God when God makes His gracious response to them, and when they respond." – positively! (*emphasis added*).

As a young man, I spent a couple of years in the British Merchant Navy, as a chef on the Orient (later P&O-Orient) Line's ss Oriana. This was, at the time one of the largest liners afloat – although, compared to some modern vessels, she was only a large lifeboat! (I do exaggerate!) – and she took me around the world many times, and enabled me to visit places that I would never, otherwise, have been able to visit.

Now, please let me emphasise that I left the MN still as sexually pure as I was when I joined. However, let's imagine that that was not the case; that I had the traditional "girl in every port" and that, through some of them, I had fathered children. Fast forward a number of years. I am now happily married, and the father of two lovely children, through my wife. So, in this scenario, I have fathered children in other parts of the world whom I have possibly never even met, and with whom I have no relationship whatsoever. I have also fathered two children for whom I have accepted full responsibility; whom I love and cherish; with whom I have formed a wonderful relationship. Do you see the difference? For those other children, I would only be a father in the sense of paternity; for the two borne to me by my wife, I am truly "father"; we have a personal relationship.

And this is one of the central truths of the Christian faith – it is <u>not</u> a set of rules and regulations by which we must live if we are to attain a certain state of bliss; it is a personal relationship with Almighty God in which He accepts us, in the Son, as His own children, and makes us partakers of His grace.

We have already noted that, concerning the Lord Jesus, John writes, in his record of the Gospel, that:

> *"He came to His own home, and His own people received Him not. But to all who received Him, who believed in His name,* **He gave power to become children of God***; who were born, not of blood, nor of the will of the flesh, nor of the will of man, but of God."* (John 1:11–13; *emphasis added*).

Now it so happens that, because the disciple responds in love to the love of God – as John later reminds us:

> *"We love, be<u>cause</u> He first loved us."* (4:19)

– he tends to live in a different way, with new attitudes. But my way of life, my service to my Lord, my "good works", are the **result** of my salvation – not the means by which I attain it! So Paul writes to the Ephesian believers:

> *"For we are His workmanship, created in Christ Jesus* **for good works***, which God prepared*

> *beforehand, that we should walk in them."* (2:10; *emphasis added*).

I am a minister of the Gospel <u>because</u> I have been saved – not in some vain kind of hope that, by so being, I might warrant a little of God's favour!

But if I become a child of God, not by works but by grace, through faith, how does this grace operate? There are three special acts of God's grace by which He makes us His children, and it is those three acts at which I want us to look now. The first is substitution, or we might use the more theological words "propitiation" and "expiation"[5] because all are concerned with the sacrifice – the acceptable sacrifice – of Jesus the Christ, on the cross, dying there on our behalf; being our substitute.

We've already noted that we are not, in a relational sense, children of God by nature. Rather, we are children of wrath, cut off from Him by our sinfulness – the sinfulness that is common to all of us:

> "… *all have sinned and fall short of the glory of God,*" (Rom 3:23).

All that we deserve is His righteous judgment and punishment:

> "*The wages of sin is death*" (Rom.6:23).

---

[5] These words are dealt with in "*Great Words of the Faith*".

Only Jesus is the Son of God by nature – the only-begotten of the Father, and, Himself, God. The wonder of the substitutionary work of God is that He makes the Son of His love to be the object of His wrath, so that the objects of His wrath might become the sons of His love!

Writing to the Corinthians, Paul put it like this:

> *"For our sake He made Him to be sin who knew no sin, so that in Him we might become the righteousness of God."* (II Cor. 5:21);

and Peter, referring to Jesus in his first letter writes:

> *"He Himself bore our sins in His body on the tree, that we might die to sin and live to righteousness."* (2:24).

So Paul can write to the believers in Rome:

> *"There is therefore now no condemnation for those who are in Christ Jesus. For the law of the Spirit of life in Christ Jesus has set me free from the law of sin and death. For God has done what the law, weakened by the flesh, could not do: sending his own Son in the likeness of sinful flesh and for sin, he condemned sin in the flesh, in order that the just requirement of the law might be fulfilled in us, who walk not according to the flesh but according to the Spirit."* (Rom 8:1-4).

No man/woman could ever have been an acceptable sacrifice; no man could ever have paid the price and penalty of the sin of mankind. Only the sinless Son of God; God the Son; could be the acceptable sacrifice – and so He took our place, yours and mine; He became our Substitute and, as we accept what He has done on our behalf, we become God's children.

> *"… He was wounded for our transgressions, He was bruised for our iniquities; upon Him was the chastisement that made us whole, and with His stripes we are healed. All we like sheep have gone astray; we have turned every one to his own way; and YHWH has laid on Him the iniquity of us all."* (Isa. 53:5-6).

"Amazing love!" wrote Charles Wesley, "how can it be that Thou, my God, shouldst die for me!?"

I love the little verse:

"That Thou shouldst love me, as I am,
and be the God Thou art;
is darkness to my intellect –
but sunshine to my heart"!

We become God's children by the gracious act of substitution; and also by the act of adoption

Writing to the Roman believers, Paul said:

> "*All who follow the leading of God's Spirit are God's own sons ... you have been adopted into the very family circle of God, and you can say with a full heart, 'Father, my Father'.*" (8:14-16; Phillips).

Writing to the fellowship in Ephesus, he said:

> "*For He chose us in Him before the creation of the world to be holy and blameless in His sight. In love He predestined us to be adopted as His sons through Jesus Christ, in accordance with His pleasure and will – to the praise of His glorious grace, which He has freely given us in the One He loves.*" (1:4-6; NIV).

Adoption speaks of a deliberate act of love. I recall reading a magazine article in which couples who had adopted children were telling of their experiences in explaining to their children that they had been adopted. The one that sticks in my mind was the case in which the parents explained to their adopted child that, while most mums and dads just had to take what they got, they had chosen their daughter out of all of the other children, because they loved her. So, as children of God, we have this assurance that we have been chosen by Him, because He loves us. Another relevant, and to me beautiful, quotation was taken from the Social Medium *Facebook*: "Adoption is when a child grows in its Mum's heart, instead of in her tummy"!

But to John's first readers, adoption had an additional aspect – a legal one. You see, under Roman law (and I believe that UK law is the same) the adopted son had equal standing with the natural son in a family. So, as His adopted children;

members of His family by His deliberate and gracious act, we have the same standing in His sight as the "natural" Son, even Jesus! Turning, yet again, to Paul's letter to the Roman believers, we find these words:

> *"... we are children of God and, if children, then heirs, heirs of God and **fellow heirs with Christ**, provided we suffer with Him in order that we may also be glorified with Him."* (8:16-17).

What an amazing privilege! In my first book, one of the 'great words' at which I look is the word 'justification', and its cognates. One of the latter is 'justified', and I explain that, when I experience the salvation that Jesus won for me, on the cross, then I am treated by Father God "just-as-if-I'd" never sinned – I am justified!

However, as a child of God, I am also adopted – and that is even more wonderful. In his book, "Knowing God", Dr James Packer writes: "Adoption is the highest privilege that the Gospel offers: higher even than justification. This may cause some raising of eyebrows, for justification is the gift of God on which, since Luther, evangelicals have laid the greatest stress. None the less, careful thought will show the truth of the statement we have just made. ... ... Adoption is higher because of the richer relationship with God that it involves. Justification is a *forensic* idea, conceived in terms of *law*, and viewing God as *judge*. In justification, God declares of penitent believers that they are not, and never will be, liable to the death that their sins deserve, because Jesus Christ, their substitute and sacrifice, tasted death in their place on the cross. ... ... Adoption is a *family* idea, conceived in terms of *love*, and viewing God as *father*. In adoption, God takes us into His family and fellowship, and establishes us as His children and heirs. Closeness, affection, and generosity are at the heart of the relationship. **To be right with God the judge is a great thing; but to be loved and cared for by God the Father is a greater**." (pps 230-231; *bold emphasis added*).

Substitution; adoption; and all is made effective by regeneration.

This simply refers to the new birth.

> "... *born of Him* ..."

was the phrase that set John off in this outburst of wonder and praise. And this is a re-birth! Jesus' words to Nicodemus, you may recall, were:

> "*Truly, truly, I say to you, unless one is born anew, he cannot see the kingdom of God.*" (John 3:3).

In adoption, we receive the privileges of God's children, and this is marvellous enough. But in regeneration, Father God goes even further, and gives us the very nature of His children. So John can say:

> "*See what love the Father has given us, that we should be called children of God;* ***and so we are.***" (3:1; *emphasis added*).

This is no mere title – it is a glorious reality! I recall, as the probationer assistant minister in a congregation in

Edinburgh, having the responsibility of leading the Bible Class. In the group of young people were two who were, I could see, brother and sister. It was not simply that the roll showed them with the same surname, and living at the same address. It was also the fact that they looked so like one another.

I decided that it would be good to visit the homes of my group and, when I visited their home, I remarked to their mother (whom I had not previously met!) that I could now see that they both looked like her. She was delighted. She then informed me that they were not even siblings; that each had been adopted when only a few weeks old. "How encouraging", she said, "that you should see such a family resemblance."

This, of course, raises the question for every one who claims to be a disciple of Jesus; a child of God; a member of the Family: have I become more like my heavenly Father?!

Son-ship has that result of changing the relationship. A friend of many years ago arrived at meeting in a newer car than the old banger that she had been driving since we had known her – and for many years previous to that! When asked what had happened, she replied: "I realised that I am a child of the King. That makes me a princess, and a princess ought to be driving a half-decent car"! We may find some fault with her logic – but there is more than a grain of truth in it! I share my first name with the current heir to the throne of the United Kingdom of Great Britain and Northern Ireland. That's where the similarity ends! His mother is HM the Queen. He has never had to worry about paying the bills; decorating the house; servicing the car. He certainly won't be sleeping on the Embankment tonight (not that I shall, either!). He is a prince of the realm.

But I, too, am a prince; more, I am a saint; even more, I am a child of the King of kings, and Lord of lords – not because of the circumstances of my physical birth, but because I have been re-born; regenerated; renewed.

> "... *born anew, not of perishable seed but of imperishable, through the living and abiding word of God;*" (I Peter 1:23).

And all of that is true for every individual who has been born again of God the Holy Spirit. We may be assured of **His** acceptance. **We** need to acknowledge **our** acceptance of that substitution; that adoption; that regeneration.

May each of us be filled with the same wonder and excitement that John had, as we contemplate that love - the:

"... amazing gift of love the Father hath bestowed on us, the sinful sons of men, to call us sons of God."! (Scottish Metrical Paraphrases, No.63).

Chapter 9.

Love – the major characteristic of the family

In the previous chapter, we looked at the outburst of wonder and praise that is found in 3:1-3. We discovered that this was brought about by John's phrase "*... born of Him.*" in what we know as the end of chap.2, and was to do with the fact that, although by nature we are merely God's creatures and, because of our sinfulness, the objects of His wrath and righteous judgment; yet, if we have committed ourselves wholly to Him, in repentance and faith, through the Lord Jesus the Christ – then we are His adopted children!

In this chapter, I want to continue along same lines, and think further of the family of God. Families often have certain characteristics – physical and behavioural. When we see a child, we often say: "He's a Paterson"; or "She's a Campbell"; or whatever. Or it may be simply, "He's his dad's double!" "She's just like her mum." It may be the colouring of the hair; the voice; some physical trait; the way in which the child acts, or walks. But whatever it may be, it identifies the child as belonging to that particular family; to those specific parents.

God's children should, likewise, be identifiable by a family characteristic – and that characteristic, says John, is love.

> "... *this is the message which you have heard from the beginning, that we should love one another,*" (3:11).

And of course, not love in merely emotional sense, but in an evaluational sense – the Greek word αγαπη.

That is to say that the one who claims to be a disciple of Jesus, should be recognisable by the worth (s)he places on individuals – simply because we know that they are also those for whom the Christ hung on a cross.

> *"Every one who commits sin is guilty of lawlessness; sin is lawlessness. You know that He appeared to take away sins, and in Him there is no sin. No one who abides in Him sins; no one who sins has either seen Him or known Him. Little children, let no one deceive you. He who does right is righteous, as He is righteous. He who commits sin is of the devil; for the devil has sinned from the beginning. The reason the Son of God appeared was to destroy the works of the devil. No one born of God commits sin; for God's nature abides in him, and he cannot sin because he is born of God. By this it may be seen who are the children of God, and who are the children of the*

devil: whoever does not do right is not of God, nor he who does not love his brother.

For this is the message which you have heard from the beginning, that we should love one another, and not be like Cain who was of the evil one and murdered his brother. And why did he murder him? Because his own deeds were evil and his brother's righteous. Do not wonder, brethren, that the world hates you. We know that we have passed out of death into life, because we love the brethren. He who does not love abides in death. Any one who hates his brother is a murderer, and you know that no murderer has eternal life abiding in him. By this we know love, that He laid down His life for us; and we ought to lay down our lives for the brethren. But if any one has the world's goods and sees his brother in need, yet closes his heart against him, how does God's love abide in him? Little children, let us not love in word or speech but in deed and in truth." (3:4-18).

In this section of the letter, John is concerned with three aspects of this family characteristic. Let's note the concern that Christian love portrays.

John makes two comments that have to do with this aspect of Christian love. The first is that it has been received personally:

"See what love the Father has given us," (3:1)

he has already written. This is not a case of God merely showing us His love – 'though that is what He did, supremely, at Calvary, and it is wonderful indeed; nor is it a case of God pouring out His love in a general fashion – 'though true that all love comes from Him; it is a case of God actually giving to His children the love that He has, the love that He is!

And this love brings with it transformed set of values. Things, and people, are viewed from a new perspective; there is a totally new attitude to everything. And attitude does make a difference! We become positive, rather than negative. If I may quote Professor Barclay, once again: "A joyless Christian is a contradiction in terms".

Some, from my own generation, may recall these words of the hymnwriter:

"Loved with everlasting love,
led by grace that love to know;
Spirit, breathing from above,
Thou hast taught me it is so.
O what full and perfect peace,
joy and wonder all divine!
In a love which cannot cease
I am His, and He is mine.

Heaven above is softer blue,
earth around is richer green;
something lives in every hue,
Christless eyes have never seen:
songs of birds in sweetness grow,
flowers with deeper beauties shine,

since I know, as now I know,
I am His and He is mine.

His for ever, His alone!
Who the Lord from me shall part?
With what joy and peace unknown
Christ can fill the loving heart!
Heaven and earth may pass away,
sun and stars in gloom decline,
but while God and I shall be:
I am His and He is mine." (George Wade Robinson)

But this love is not only an experience of which the disciple of Jesus should be aware; it is also an evidence by which the disciple of Jesus may be assured.

> *"We know that we have passed out of death into life, because we love …"* (v.14)

This a very significant verse. Assurance of salvation is ours when we realise that our values **are** changing – the Word of God; the house of God; the people of God; the Lord's day; all of these, and more, are now valued whereas, before, we considered them to be boring, and dull! And if this isn't true for any one of us, then I honestly believe that we should be questioning, very closely, our claims to be disciples of Jesus!

This love of God that we are called to portray will be received personally; but it will also be revealed practically.

True Christian love is never content to remain inactive. It longs to act; to serve; to minister; to do! So John exhorts:

> *"My children, let us not love not merely in theory or in words – let us love in sincerity and in practice."* (v.18; Phillips);
>
> *"My children, our love is not to be just words or mere talk, but something real and active."* (J.B.);
>
> *"… it must be true love, which shows itself in action."* (GNB).

Of course, John is not alone in encouraging such action. Listen to James:

> *"… be doers of the word, and not hearers only, deceiving yourselves. For if any one is a hearer of the word and not a doer, he is like a man who observes his natural face in a mirror; for he observes himself and goes away and at once forgets what he was like. But he who looks into the perfect law, the law of liberty, and perseveres, being no hearer that forgets but a doer that acts, he shall be blessed in his doing."* (1:22-25).

And, of course, the whole of what we know as James 2 majors on the practicalities of being a believer.

Paul, who some seem to think thought of nothing but grace and faith, reminds his friends in Ephesus that:

> *"… we are His workmanship, created in Christ Jesus **for good works,** which God prepared beforehand, that we should walk in them."* (2:10; *emphasis added*).

And the Lord Jesus, Himself said:

> *"Let your light so shine before men, that they may see your good works and give glory to your Father Who is in heaven."* (Matt 5:16).

This is the example that the Father has given.

> *"God so loved the world that He gave ..."*;

He acted. And John, who recorded those words, reminds us, here that

> *"By this we know love, that He laid down His life for us;"*

and he continues:

> *"... and we ought to lay down our lives for the brethren."* (v.16).

Christian love; αγαπη love; is a sacrificial love.

I recall an occasion when a fellow-minister in the Presbytery of which I was a member at the time, was leaving to go to a different parish. As was customary, a member of the congregation he was leaving paid tribute to him. The memorable part of the tribute concerned the thorny subject of financial giving. Apparently, his response to some concerns from the members of the congregation that the amount that was being requested from "Central Offices" was too much, ended: "This is one true avenue to give outside our parish area. Give smilingly; give until it hurts; **and then give some more**"! That, I would suggest, was Christian love speaking – love that is revealed in a most practical manner; love that portrays genuine concern.

John speaks of the concern that Christian love portrays; and then he speaks of the conduct that Christian love pursues.

Christian love; αγαπη love; the love of a true disciple of Jesus; not only effects our attitudes and actions towards God, and towards others, but also towards ourselves!

John speaks of how different the child of God will be.

In v.9, he makes an amazing statement:

> "*No one born of God commits sin; for God's nature abides in him, and he cannot sin because he is born of God.*"

At first sight, this seems a wee bit extreme – if not downright impossible! Is John saying that, if I sin – and sin I do – then I am not a child of God? Does this not contradict what he has written earlier about the possibility of a Christian sinning? (1:8-10).

The problem is, as is so often the case, one of language. John is using, here, a tense (Present Continuous) that doesn't formally exist in the English language. Prof. Barclay translates more accurately when he renders the Greek text as:

> "*… he cannot be a consistent and deliberate sinner.*"

A disciple of Jesus cannot, and does not, go on and on continually persisting in sin, and 'enjoying' to the full a life of disobedience and rebellion against God. I remind you, again, of the story of the pig, the sheep, and the muddy pool!

When a disciple of Jesus does sin, it is against his nature, as a child of God; and so he can never enjoy it – he isn't content until he gets out of it. And the closer we get to God, the more we see our sin for what it is, and the more we abhor it. It's a reversal of the jeweller's ploy! Diamond looks much better when set against black velvet cloth. It's all to do with contrast. The black background makes the diamond appear to sparkle more than would a white background. Similarly, the closer I get to Father God; the more easily I see my sins against His perfection and purity; the more heinous they are shown to be, and the more quickly I want the relationship with Him, that is mine, to be restored.

But there is a danger if we use such verses as an excuse for sinning or for taking sin too lightly. If the question is asked "*Can* a Christian not sin?" then the answer is yes! God indeed, in Christ, has made every provision necessary for a believer never to commit sin, and we are without any legitimate excuse whenever we do.

This must be so for at least two reasons. In the first place, Jesus Christ in His humanity is our example, and He

> "... *was in all points tempted like as we are, yet without sin*" (Heb. 4:15).

He accomplished this, not because of His deity, but solely in His humanity.

Secondly, God has *commanded* us not to sin, and He would never command us to do the impossible. For every temptation, there is a way of escape:

> *"No temptation has overtaken you that is not common to man. God is faithful, and he will not let you be tempted beyond your strength, but with the temptation will also provide the way of escape, that you may be able to endure it."* (I Cor.10:13),

and we have no excuse if we fail to take it. Our only recourse is to repent and confess the sin.

How different the child of God will be; but how despised the child of God will be.

> *"Do not wonder, brethren, that the world hates you."*,

writes John (v.13). And *"the world"*, we have discovered in earlier chapters, is "human society insofar as it is organised on wrong principles, and characterised by base desires, false values, and egoism." (C.H.Dodd). It is, quite simply, mankind without God! And the reason why the world hates, and despises, the disciple of Jesus is simply that the disciple, by his/her different values and attitudes, is passing judgement on the world!

John illustrates this by his reference to Cain:

> *"For this is the message which you have heard from the beginning, that we should love one another, and not be like Cain who was of the evil one and murdered his brother. And why did he murder him?*

> *Because his own deeds were evil and his brother's righteous."* (vs.11-12).

Remember, this is a pastoral letter, in which John is dealing with situations being experienced by the flock. It may be that some were astonished that they should be persecuted for doing good! At the time of writing, there is, in a jail in Pakistan, a woman named Asya – and she is under sentence of death! What, then, is the terrible crime that she committed? Nothing more than sharing a cup of water with fellow-workers in the field in which she and they were employed as labourers! However, Asya is a disciple of Jesus; her co-workers were Muslims; and they accused her of blasphemy – a 'crime' which, in Pakistan, does carry the death penalty.

Abel's only 'crime' was to present an offering that God found more acceptable than Cain's. And the latter slew his own blood brother – one of only four human beings alive at that time!

But, of course, this hatred was foretold by the Lord Jesus, Himself, as John records in his account of the Gospel message:

> *"If the world hates you, know that it has hated Me before it hated you. ... ... Remember the word that I said to you, 'A servant is not greater than his master.' If they persecuted Me, they will persecute you;"* (John 15:18, 20).

Christian love, then, portrays a particular concern; it pursues a particular conduct; and it provides a particular contrast.

And, just as the conduct is born of the concern, so the contrast is born of the conduct. In "*the world*", John sees the life that rejects the law of God; that wants to do its own thing. It harks back to the situation in Israel at the end of the period of the judges:

> "*In those days there was no king in Israel;* ***every man did what was right in his own eyes.***" (Judges 21:25; *emphasis added*).

And that, in one word, is sin – the consistent, continual, deliberate breaking of the law of God. John describes such people very simply, and without any 'beating about the bush'! They are, he says,

> "*… children of the devil …*" (v.10).

No "political correctness" there!

Of course, Jesus used a similar term on one occasion, again recorded by John in his account of the Gospel. Some Jews had paid lip-service to Him; had claimed to believe in Him (v.31), even as we claim to believe in Him! But they had failed to back up their profession by their behaviour. So Jesus told them, quite bluntly:

> "*You are of your father the devil, …*" (John 8:39).

How many there are today who, while claiming by their profession of membership of a Christian fellowship to be

God's children, show by their practical rejection of Him, and His law, that they are in fact, children of the devil?!

Augustine wrote: "For all who do not love God are strangers, antichrists. And though they come to the churches, they cannot be numbered among the children of God; the fountain of life does not belong to them. To have baptism is possible even for a bad man; to have prophecy is possible even for a bad man. We find that King Saul had prophecy: he was persecuting holy David, yet he was filled with the spirit of prophecy, and began to prophesy. To receive the sacrament of the body and blood of the Lord is possible even for a bad man: for of such it is said, "he that eats and drinks unworthily eats and drinks judgement to himself". To have the name of Christ is possible even for a bad man; i.e. even a bad man can be called a Christian: as those of whom it is said, "*they polluted the name of their God*". I say, to have all the sacraments is possible even for a bad man; but to have love and to be a bad man, is not possible.

"… once for all, then, a short precept is given to you: love, and do what you will: whether you hold your peace, through love hold your peace; whether you cry out, through love cry out; whether you correct, through love correct; whether you spare, through love spare: let the root of love be within, of this route can nothing spring but what is good." (Augustine, 1 John; Homily 7).

But, in contrast to these people whose lives reject the law of God, there are those in whose lives may be seen the love that respects the law of God.

Love for a person involves loving, and caring for, the things that that person loves and cares for. It involves respecting that which the person holds as precious and important. And those who truly love Father God respect His law. We love what He loves, and desire to know what will please Him, so that we may go and do it. We repeat the words of Jesus, in the Garden of Gethsemane:

"... *not My will, but Yours, be done.*" (Lk 22:42).

Listen, again, to Augustine: "Once for all, then, a short precept is given thee: Love, and do what thou wilt: whether thou hold thy peace, through love hold thy peace; whether thou cry out, through love cry out; whether thou correct, through love correct; whether thou spare, through love do thou spare: let the root of love be within, of this root can nothing spring but what is good." (1 John; Homily 7).

Love: the family characteristic of the children of God. It's the

"fruit of the Spirit" (Gal.5:22),

that manifests itself in

"*... joy, peace, patience, kindness, goodness, faithfulness, gentleness, self-control;*" (Gal 5:22-23).

But that begs the question, does it not – is that characteristic really seen in your life, and in mine? If we claim to be disciples of Jesus; if we come to His Table, and partake of the elements that symbolise His body and blood – and do so **in obedience to His command to do so** - then it should be, and we give to Him all the thanksgiving and praise that are His due, for having accepted us, in the Lord Jesus, into His family.

But what if that love is not seen in our lives? Then surely, now is the time to open our hearts to the life-giving power of Holy Spirit, that He might enter in, make us true children of the Father, and so work in us that that love will grow, and blossom, and flourish.

And to our great Triune God, Father, Son, and Holy Spirit, we will give all the praise, and glory, and honour, world without end. Hallelujah!

Chapter 10.

The confidence of the child of God.

This chapter brings us within sight of end of our getting to know this wonderful letter, and it is my hope, and prayer, that you will feel that you have come to deeper understanding of what John is saying here, and realised that it is as relevant to us in these early years of the 21st century, A.D., as it was to those to whom it was first written. Through that, I trust that you will have come to a deeper knowledge of, and love for, John's Saviour and Lord – and mine!

We look, in this chapter, at another longer passage – 3:19 – 4:6

> *"No one born of God commits sin; for God's nature abides in him, and he cannot sin because he is born of God. By this it may be seen who are the children of God, and who are the children of the devil:*

whoever does not do right is not of God, nor he who does not love his brother.

For this is the message which you have heard from the beginning, that we should love one another, and not be like Cain who was of the evil one and murdered his brother. And why did he murder him? Because his own deeds were evil and his brother's righteous. Do not wonder, brethren, that the world hates you. We know that we have passed out of death into life, because we love the brethren. He who does not love abides in death. Anyone who hates his brother is a murderer, and you know that no murderer has eternal life abiding in him. By this we know love, that He laid down His life for us; and we ought to lay down our lives for the brethren. But if anyone has the world's goods and sees his brother in need, yet closes his heart against him, how does God's love abide in him? Little children, let us not love in word or speech but in deed and in truth.

By this we shall know that we are of the truth, and reassure our hearts before Him whenever our hearts condemn us; for God is greater than our hearts, and he knows everything. Beloved, if our hearts do not condemn us, we have confidence before God; and we receive from Him whatever we ask, because we keep

His commandments and do what pleases Him. And this is His commandment, that we should believe in the Name of His Son Jesus Christ and love one another, just as He has commanded us. All who keep His commandments abide in Him, and He in them. And by this we know that He abides in us, by the Spirit which He has given us.

Beloved, do not believe every spirit, but test the spirits to see whether they are of God; for many false prophets have gone out into the world. By this you know the Spirit of God: every spirit which confesses that Jesus Christ has come in the flesh is of God, and every spirit which does not confess Jesus is not of God. This is the spirit of antichrist, of which you heard that it was coming, and now it is in the world already. Little children, you are of God, and have overcome them; for He who is in you is greater than he who is in the world. They are of the world, therefore what they say is of the world, and the world listens to them. We are of God. Whoever knows God listens to us, and he who is not of God does not listen to us. By this we know the spirit of truth and the spirit of error."

One commentator on the letter writes of "the uncompromising rigour" of John's "definitions and tests of spiritual genuineness". (John Stott). John was very much a "black and white" man. He didn't try to negotiate some middle way. His themes are light and darkness; life and death; truth and lies; children of God and children of the devil; and more. I would suggest that one of the many problems in the church, certainly in the west, in our day, is a lack of such uncompromising rigour. All too often it's become a case of "anything goes" – and appointments are made, even appointments to leadership, without any recourse to Biblical standards! The suggestion is made that these "hard words" must have constrained many of the original readers to ask, in the words of the earlier disciples:

"*Who then can be saved?*" (Mt.19:25).

So we find what has been referred to as the "balance" of the letter – that with the ministry of exhortation comes a ministry of encouragement.

J.B. Phillips, in his helpful translation of the N.T., entitles this section "Living in love means confidence in God", and it is confidence that is our main theme in this chapter – the confidence of love, and of knowledge.

Confidence is always a mark of love and of knowledge. How confidently will a child approach its father with a request; while a stranger might approach the same man, with a request, with hesitation? How confidently would a child make its way about its own home; while a stranger would be uncertain as to which door led to which room?

Let's consider, then, as we look at the closing verses of what we know as chapter 3, where we may see the confidence we may have before the throne of God.

In v.21 John affirms that

> "... *we have confidence before God;*"

However, as is so often the case, there is a condition attached:

> "*Beloved, **if our hearts do not condemn us,** we have confidence before God;*" (*emphasis added*)

But in what sort of circumstance do our hearts **not** condemn us?! John provides the answer to that question with the simple – yet profound – statement:

> "... *we keep His commandments and do what pleases Him.*"

This, in turn, he reminds us, involves

> "... *that we should believe in the Name of His Son Jesus Christ and love one another,*".

This "belief", of course, is not mere mental assent. It is the belief that may be thought of as trust – in the way that, if going into hospital for a major operation, I might say that "I believe in my surgeon". I am saying, effectively, that I trust this person – even to the extent of placing my life in his/her hands!

So we see that there are two conditions that must be fulfilled. The first of these concerns a choice that must have been made. A choice in which my faith, and trust, and dependence, and reliance, are placed in and on the Person of Jesus, the Christ. It's a choice in which I accept the authority and Lordship of that same Jesus, and become obedient to Him with that obedience that is really what lies at the heart of a valid conversion experience. And, of course, it is this choice – this entering freely into a vital relationship with Jesus, that makes a person a Christian: a disciple of Jesus. It's not some church ritual; it's not where I was born; it's not my family tree; it's not my status in society – or in the church. It's all to do with Jesus, and with Him alone.

But, tied in with that choice, is a change that will be manifest. One of the mistakes that many make is of "trying to be" a Christian. They do this, that, and the other 'good works'; this, that, and the other commendable action; and hope that Father God will be sufficiently impressed to smile favourably upon them!

But this simply isn't the way in which God works. I became a Christian; a disciple of Jesus; by making a choice, and entering into a new relationship with Jesus, the Christ. But that relationship meant that I had to change my attitudes – not simply towards God, but towards everything, and everyone. And this is a change that must be seen – or my claim to be one of His followers should be questioned. It's a change that may best be described as "a new love"; a new evaluation of persons and things; a seeing through God's eyes. It's the second verse of that song I quoted in the previous chapter:

"Heaven above is softer blue,
earth around is richer green;
something lives in every hue,
Christless eyes have never seen:
songs of birds in sweetness grow,
flowers with deeper beauties shine,
since I know, as now I know,
I am His and He is mine."

Beauty, we are told, is in the eye of the beholder. People see others through the rose-tinted spectacles of love. I know that if I were to stand my wife beside some young model, and they were to be looked at totally objectively, then the model would be considered, by most, to be the more "beautiful". But then, I don't look at my wife in such an objective fashion. She is my wife – and I still fancy her!

And, of course, that change should be seen, and heard, in my actions and my words; in the people with whom I spend my time, and the places in which I spend my time. There will be new priorities – and spending time with my Lord, whether in my private devotions, or in fellowship with others, will be at the top of my list. If I am obliged to make a choice between satisfying some personal desire, and learning more about Him – and getting to know Him better! – then there will be no contest!

There are conditions that must be fulfilled and, until they are, there can be no valid confidence before Almighty God. But, for those who have made this choice; in whose lives this change is manifest; those who can say, with John,

"… *we have confidence before God.*",

there is also a communion that should be enjoyed.

If we have entered into this new relationship with God, in Christ Jesus, and through the indwelling power of God the Holy Spirit, then we are children of God and, as such, we have the openness, the frankness, the readiness of access to God's presence, and the assurance of the Father's welcome for His child! This is one of the joys of being a disciple of Jesus – that I have this tremendous assurance that Almighty God, the Creator and Sustainer of all that is, is my Father, and that I can enjoy a real communion with Him.

John writes about two facets of this communion. He notes how it can be clouded.

John Stott comments: "However firmly grounded the Christian's assurance is, his heart may sometimes need reassurance. Indeed," he says "if the RSV is correct in translating the first phrase of v.20 '*whenever our hearts condemn us*', the suggestion seems to be that it may not be either an unusual, or an infrequent, experience for the Christian's serene assurance to be disturbed."

What does that mean? Simply that, as a disciple of Jesus, I am going to be constantly targeted by the enemy, and he is going to accentuate my failings. There are times when my communion with my Heavenly Father is clouded; times when my confidence is replaced by a sense of condemnation that arises out of a knowledge of my own sin and rebelliousness. And the need then arises to persuade my heart – sometimes with great difficulty – that I can, and may, and must still look up into the face of my loving Father.

You see, as we are reminded by the prophet Jeremiah,

> "... *the heart is deceitful above all things, and desperately wicked;*" (17:9)

and it can accuse me wrongly. But Jeremiah goes on to ask, regarding the heart

> "*who can know it?*"

and the glorious answer to that question is "God can, and does, know it!" I may, under the influence of the enemy, accuse myself falsely – but Father God will never (not ever!) make a mistake. As we walk in love, and with our hearts open to Him Who is love, we may come to Him in spite of the accusations of the accuser, the satan.

No Christian should treat sin lightly, but no Christian should be harder on himself than God is. There is a morbid kind of self-examination and self-condemnation that is neither spiritual nor Biblical. Once you confess your sin and it is forgiven **and forgotten** by Father God, you need not allow it to accuse you anymore.

> "*There is therefore **now no condemnation** for those who are in Christ Jesus.*" (Rom.8:1; *emphasis added*).

So John writes of how the clouding can be cleared.

He has spoken of the condemnation of my own heart; but he is also able to say that

> "... *God is greater than our hearts, and he knows everything.*" (3:20).

It is true that those words may be interpreted as meaning that if our hearts condemn us, and God is infinitely greater than our hearts, then how much more will He condemn us! If we take it like that, then we are left with nothing but the fear of God – and not the reverential fear that is right and proper, but the "scaredy" fear that is a negative emotion – and the inevitable condemnation of God that leaves us with nothing to say other than "God, be merciful to me, a sinner"! But I would suggest that that is not what John is saying, in context, for here he is thinking of our confidence **in** God, not our dread **of** God.

So what John is saying here is that God, knowing all things, does not – like our accusing hearts (through which the satan speaks) – take notice only of our inconsistencies and failures; the battles lost; the weak evasions of our duty; our faltering faith. He takes equal note of the struggle, and the attempting; of the prayers, and the penitence, and the shame; of the going out into the night and weeping bitterly, that proves how passionate is the loyalty we so cravenly denied. That was Simon Peter's experience. (Mt.26:75).

Our hearts, as human creatures, can only judge by what we see and hear. But Almighty God judges by what He knows! What He knows, not only about the past, but also about the future; about the lessons that have been learned; about the sympathy that will have been deepened (Heb.4:16); the pride that will have been broken; the lives that are still to be won. He is Omniscient – He knows **all** things – and in His perfect knowledge is our hope and our confidence.

There is a confidence that we may have before the throne of God and in His presence. And then in the opening verses of chap.4, we find John speaking about the confidence we may have about the truth of God.

Here, he speaks, not of the confidence that is based on a loving relationship, but of the confidence that is based on a living knowledge.

He warns, first of all, that there are other spirits – that not every supernatural experience is from God. I remember well, the personal discovery that the devil can counterfeit the gifts of God the Holy Spirit! Of course, what he is totally unable to counterfeit is the fruit of the Spirit which is Love!

So there is a distortion of the truth that the disciple of Jesus will meet.

Writing to the Ephesian believers, Paul said:

> "*For we are not contending against flesh and blood, but against the principalities, against the powers, against the world rulers of this present darkness, against the spiritual hosts of wickedness in the heavenly places.*" (6:12).

The Life Application Bible offers this translation:

> "*For we are not fighting against people made of flesh and blood, but against persons without bodies – the evil rulers of the unseen world, those mighty satanic beings and great evil princes of darkness who rule this world; and against huge numbers of wicked spirits in the spirit world.*"

These are not people, but fallen angels over whom the satan has control. Note that the word "devil" refers to him as the accuser; "satan", on the other hand, means "adversary". He is not compared to a lion and a dragon just for fun! Never underestimate his power – it is much greater than ours! But, at the same time, never forget that

> "... *He who is in you is greater than he who is in the world.*" (4:4).

These are not mere fantasies; they are very real. We face a powerful enemy with the single goal of defeating the church, and the chosen people. This, I would contend, is the reason why most "religious" persecution is against Jews and Christians!

Before we were converted, the devil didn't need to bother about us. We were his children! But the moment we came to the Lord Jesus, in repentance and faith, and accepted the salvation that He gained at such great cost at Calvary, and were adopted into the family of Almighty God, with the Lord Jesus as our elder Brother, the situation changed. He, and his cohorts, became our enemies – and they try everything to turn us away from God, and back to sin. And, although we are assured of victory, we must engage in the struggle until the Lord calls us home, or to meet with Him in the air. I have to confess to getting annoyed with those who imply – or state openly – that the life of the disciple of Jesus is for old people, children, and wimps. Any dead fish can float downstream – bit it takes a strong salmon to swim against the current as it fights its way to its spawning ground. This is why Paul provides the Ephesians with an inventory of the spiritual armour that we need to wear constantly.

We are, whether or not we realise it, in the midst of a "War of the Worlds" that H.G. Wells could never have fully depicted – even the war between good and evil. Now it is gloriously true that, at Calvary, the decisive battle was won for good – but the mopping-up continues, and will do until our victorious King returns to the battle-field (planet Earth) to claim the victory that is already His. We may compare the difference between D-day; VE-day; and VJ-day.

The evil one is out to deceive and destroy; he still hopes that, by cunning and subterfuge, he will vanquish some of the King's followers. He sends out his false prophets – wolves in sheep's clothing – even as Jesus sends out His disciples. The devil and his followers delight in half-truths; distorted truths; and in downright lying. He can quote the Bible as well as – and often better than! – any disciple of Jesus. But it is usually a misquote, or a quote taken out of context!

> *"There is no God"!* (Ps.14:1; 53:1)

sounds like the dream text of the avowed atheist! However, read in context …!!!

What a warning John gives – and it is needed just as much today as it was then. Indeed, it could be argued that it is even more necessary today, in a culture that is largely ignorant of the Word! But to be forewarned is to be forearmed. How may we tell the difference between spirits?

> *"… every spirit which confesses that Jesus Christ has come in the flesh is of God, and every spirit which does not confess Jesus is not of God."* (4:2-3).

Here we may find ourselves thinking of a discernment of the truth that the disciple of Jesus will need.

If it is indeed true that I am going to meet up with distorted truth, how am I to recognise it for what it is? Simply by applying the test! It's a test that is given to us in its most direct form by Jesus Himself Who, when certain Pharisees were gathered together, asked them a question:

"*What do you think of the Christ?*" (Mt.22:42).

This is the test to be applied to all of the claims, and counter-claims. C.S.Lewis wrote: "I am trying here to prevent anyone saying the really foolish thing that people often say about Him: I'm ready to accept Jesus as a great moral teacher, but I don't accept his claim to be God. That is the one thing we must not say. A man who was merely a man and said the sort of things Jesus said would not be a great moral teacher. He would either be a lunatic — on the level with the man who says he is a poached egg — or else he would be the Devil of Hell. You must make your choice. Either this man was, and is, the Son of God, or else a madman or something worse. You can shut him up for a fool, you can spit at him and kill him as a demon or you can fall at his feet and call him Lord and God, but let us not come with any patronizing nonsense about his being a great human teacher. He has not left that open to us. He did not intend to." (Mere Christianity; pps 52-53).

If someone tells me that Jesus was just a great teacher; or a great moralist; or a disembodied spirit; or a mere revolutionary (who failed!); I have Scriptural warrant for telling that person that (s)he is not a disciple of Jesus! A religious person, perhaps, but not a Biblical Christian. We need to remember – or, in some cases, to learn – that everything that is "religious" is not necessarily Christian, or even divine. It could be devilish! We need to be aware that not even everything that bears the name of the Christ is necessarily of Him. It could be satanic! Wherever you get a genuine and valuable article, you inevitably have someone produce a counterfeit. This is no less true in the spiritual realm. The acid test of those who claim to be Christian is

"What do you think of the Christ?",

and "Are you living your life accordingly?" It is in this very point that the modern religious sects – Mormonism, Jehovah's Witnesses, Christian Scientists, and others – fall flat: in the place they give to Him. But if we do give to Him the first place; the pre-eminent place; then we can have confidence that He will, as He promised, give to us the Spirit of Truth, Who will guide us into all truth. (Jn.16:13).

Confidence before the throne of God; confidence about the truth of God. What a wonderful thought! What a wonderful God in Whom to have confidence – the omnipotent God Who, John assures us, is greater than the devil. Is our confidence in Him? If we are His children, then it ought to be! If it isn't – if we are still depending on ourselves, or on our good works, or on our church attendance and rituals – then that suggests, strongly, that we are not, in fact, His children!

If that is the case for you, dear reader, then you need to come to Him, in repentance and faith, and receive new life in and through Him. Then will you have that confidence, and be able to bring glory to His Name.

Chapter 11.

The nature, and character, of Almighty God.

You may recall that, at the beginning, I pointed out that, as Eric Alexander described it, I John is like a spiral staircase that, while covering the same area of ground time and time again, does so at an ever-rising height.

In this chapter, we return to the test of eternal life which is found in our loving one another. We first met this test in the second chapter where, in v.10, John writes:

> "*He who loves his brother abides in the light ...*",

i.e. that love in the Christian sense – αγαπη (agapē) love: this new attitude to, and evaluation of, both people and things – is a sure sign that we are disciples of Jesus; that we are abiding in the Christ. And then we saw, when we looked at the first 18 verses of chap.3, that love is, indeed, the family characteristic of God's children – those of us who are adopted and, of course, the only-begotten Himself.

Here, in the first section of this passage, we find the same theme – but at an even higher level. For here, love is compared to the Ultimate – even to the nature and character of Almighty God Himself. J.B. Phillips heads the section, vs 7-12, with the words: "Let us love: God has shown us love at its highest". And this, of course, is challenge that comes to every adopted child of God: not merely to have, in love, the confidence of the children of God; but to love as God loves, and because God loves, and because He has shown love at its highest.

John expands this thought of the very ground of our loving by pointing out, first of all, that we should love because this is what God is like in His nature.

> *"Beloved, let us love one another; for love is of God, …",*

he writes in v.7. That is to say, God is the very source of love – without Him, it could not exist! Then, in v.8, and again in v.16, John makes the simple, but amazingly profound statement:

> *"God is love".*

In other words, love is the very essence of God Himself and, just as I've stated that without God, love could not exist, we may also say, with all reverence, that without love, God would not exist! And if that first thought is staggering, then the second is, surely, almost beyond our comprehension! But all that we are saying here is that God and love are so bound up that they must exist together, or not at all!

What I am not saying is that God is merely the highest form of love; that He is, as it were, the top rung of a ladder called 'Love' while we are on the lower rungs. Rather, it is that He is the ladder, and that any love that we may have, and express, must be seen in its relationship to Him.

The word used for 'love' is, of course, as it is throughout the New Testament, that special word, "αγαπη". It's a word that isn't found in the extant works of any of the classical authors, so John is speaking of something that is exclusive to God. It expresses the highest, the purest, the noblest form of love – the love that sees something infinitely precious in its object.

Human love tends to have two characteristics – it is roused by something in its object; it is, if you like, a response to something. And, of course, it always includes the desire to get as well as give; it is never totally unselfish.

But God's love is roused by nothing outside itself and, therefore, it is able to love the unlovely and the unlovable. And God's love is all give – He has loved me from the beginning, even when my love for Him was non-existent.

> "… *he who loves* [like this] *is born of God and knows God.*"

writes John. The Amplified Bible reads, in this verse:

> "… *he who loves [his fellowmen] is begotten (born) of God and is coming [progressively] to know and understand God [to perceive and recognize and get a better and clearer knowledge of Him].*"

In other words, when this love is seen in a human heart, it is a sign of new birth; when I can love even the unlovely, it is an indication that I am God's child.

Of course, every coin has two sides, and the obverse of what John has just written – the other side of the coin – is, as he quickly points out, that

> "*He who does not love* [in this way] *does not know God.*" (v.8).

John Stott writes: "The argument is plain and compelling. For the loveless Christian to profess to know God and to have been born of God, is like claiming to be intimate with a foreigner whose language we cannot speak, or to have been born of parents whom we do not, in any way, resemble." That is to say, that to claim God as Father in a relational sense – to have been born of Him; and as Friend – claiming to know Him; is totally empty and meaningless – if we do not love.

Remember Paul, writing to the believers in Corinth?

> *"If I speak with the tongues of men and of angels, but have no love, I become no more than blaring brass or crashing cymbal. If I have the gift of foretelling the future, and hold in my mind not only all human knowledge, but* [also] *the very secrets of God, and if I have that absolute faith which can move mountains, but have no love, I amount to nothing at all. If I dispose of all that I possess, yes, even if I give my own body to be burned, but have no love, I achieve precisely nothing."* (I Cor.13:1-3; Phillips).

We're back to the difference between the Gifts of Holy Spirit, and the Fruit of Holy Spirit. The first – the Gifts – may be counterfeited by the enemy; the second – the Fruit – cannot, because Love is the very nature of Almighty God.

And that, says John, is the reason why we should love – because love is God's eternal nature. But, more than that, it is His historical Gift.

This is how He has revealed Himself in the Son. And we may know this, because God has manifest it to us. There is an important spiritual truth here: that if we are to know Christian love – the very love of God shown in our hearts and lives – then we must start, not from the human side, but from the Divine.

> *"In this is love, not that we loved God but that He loved us and sent His Son to be the expiation for our sins."* (v.10).

Now, if you are reading the AV/KJV you will see the word "propitiation" instead of the word "expiation". Of course, to most folk – even mature believers – one is as meaningless as the other! Both words do, satisfactorily, translate the Greek word "hilasterion" which, in turn, is the word used to translate the Hebrew "kapporeth" – the word that refers to the Mercy Seat that formed the lid of the Ark of the Covenant. In the relevant chapter in *Great Words of the Faith*, I write: "Propitiation literally means "to make favourable" and specifically includes the idea of dealing with God's wrath against sinners. Expiation literally means "to make amends" and implies either the removal or cleansing of sin." Further on I write: "We might sum it up – although to do so in a sentence or two is not doing the subject anything like full justice – by saying that expiation has the sense of a sacrifice that satisfies God's legal requirements, while propitiation has the sense of a sacrifice that satisfies the requirements of God's character. Expiation refers to that which is judicial; propitiation refers to that which is relational. Expiation removes a barrier; propitiation removes a barrier, and restores a relationship."

However, the wonder of this act of God – and it is wholly, and solely His act – is that we who are, by nature, the objects only of His wrath and judgment, become the objects of His love. And how does this come about? Through Jesus, His only-begotten Son, the Object of His love, becoming the objects of His wrath as He bore our sins upon His own Body on the cross at Calvary; as He actually became sin (II Cor.5:21) – the very epitome/embodiment of sin; even the personification of sin – as He took our place. He became our Substitute.

In v.11 John shares with us the conclusion he draws:

> *"Beloved, if God so loved us, we also ought to love one another."*

God's love, revealed supremely in the Christ, is the mainspring of Christian love. Turning again to John Stott, he comments: "The gift of God's Son not only assures us of God's love for us, but lays upon us an obligation. No-one who has been to the cross and seen God's immeasurable and unmerited love displayed there, can go back to a life of selfishness. Indeed, the implication seems to be that 'if God so loved us, even also – in like manner and to a like degree of self-sacrifice – ought we to love one another."

We ought to love because love is God's eternal nature; because it is His historical gift; and because it is His present activity.

"No man has ever seen God;" writes John in v.12. But

> *"… if we love one another, God abides in us and His love is perfected in us."*

What the apostle is saying is that we ought to love one another because this is the continuing way in which God reveals Himself – through His people. What a privilege! The Living God, Who has revealed Himself, historically, in Christ Jesus – Mashiach Yeshua – reveals Himself contemporarily in His people: when they love one another! And this is the responsibility that accompanies the privilege! The only way in which the world will see God is through us

– and then, only as we love one another. And this reciprocal love is - staggering thought - the very perfecting of the love of God! Do you see what John is saying here? That without our loving one another, the love of God in us is not complete!

However, it must be noted that we are not referring here to nothing other than some kind of lovey-dovey, emotional, feeling. Discipline is also an expression of love, and this is a simple fact that is declared throughout the written Word of God:

> "*My son, do not despise the* LORD*'s discipline or be weary of His reproof, for the* LORD *reproves him whom He loves, as a father the son in whom he delights.*" (Prov.3:11-12);
>
> "*Besides this, we have had earthly fathers to discipline us and we respected them. Shall we not much more be subject to the Father of spirits and live? For they disciplined us for a short time at their pleasure, but He disciplines us for our good, that we may share His holiness. For the moment all discipline seems painful rather than pleasant; later it yields the peaceful fruit of righteousness to those who have been trained by it.*" (Heb.12:9-11);

to provide just two examples.

So John uses these three great truths about the love of God as an inducement to brotherly love. We are to love one another; we are to love all those whom God loves; we are to love them as God loves them. And we are to do so because He is love (vs.8,16); because He first loved us (v.19); and because, as we do, He dwells in us, and

> "… *His love is perfected in us.*" (v.12).

John then draws this section of his letter to a close by pointing out that a further assurance of God's dwelling in us is the gift of God the Holy Spirit (v.13), and the acknowledgment of Jesus as the very Son of God (v.15). And all of this will affect our attitudes, first of all Godward.

> *"There is no fear in love, but perfect love casts out fear. For fear has to do with punishment, and he who fears is not perfected in love."*

If we have this divine love in our hearts, then our attitude towards God is one of confidence, rather than fear. This is particularly relevant with regard to the Day of Judgement. So John writes, in the previous verse:

> *"… we may have confidence for the day of judgment …"*

And this is true because of the freedom that love bestows, particularly freedom of speech! In chap.3:21-22, we discovered that the disciple of Jesus has freedom of speech before the throne of grace;

> *"Beloved, if our hearts do not condemn us, we have confidence before God; and we receive from Him whatever we ask, because we keep His commandments and do what pleases Him."*

But here, we find that the disciple of Jesus can have that same boldness at the throne of judgment. Paul had already written:

> *"There is therefore now no condemnation for those who are in Christ Jesus."* (Rom.8:1).

"No condemnation now I dread; Jesus, and all in Him, is mine!
Alive **in Him**, my living Head, and clothed in **righteousness divine**;
Bold I approach the eternal throne and claim the crown, **through Christ** my own." (Charles Wesley; *emphases added*).

The unbeliever, when he stands before Almighty God, the Righteous Judge, on that day, will have no valid excuse that he can make.

> *"For what can be known about God is plain to them, because God has shown it to them. Ever since the creation of the world his invisible nature, namely, his eternal power and deity, has been clearly perceived in the things that have been made. So they are without excuse; for although they knew God they did not honour him as God or give thanks to him, but they became futile in their thinking and their senseless minds were darkened. Claiming to be wise, they became fools, and exchanged the glory of the immortal God for images resembling mortal man or birds or animals or reptiles.*
>
> *Therefore God gave them up in the lusts of their hearts to impurity, to the dishonouring of their bodies among themselves, because they exchanged the truth about God for a lie and worshiped and served the creature rather than the Creator, Who is blessed for ever! Amen.*
>
> *For this reason God gave them up to dishonourable passions. Their women exchanged natural relations for unnatural, and the men likewise gave up natural relations with women and were consumed with passion for one another, men committing shameless*

> *acts with men and receiving in their own persons the due penalty for their error.*
>
> *And since they did not see fit to acknowledge God, God gave them up to a base mind and to improper conduct. They were filled with all manner of wickedness, evil, covetousness, malice. Full of envy, murder, strife, deceit, malignity, they are gossips, slanderers, haters of God, insolent, haughty, boastful, inventors of evil, disobedient to parents, foolish, faithless, heartless, ruthless. Though they know God's decree that those who do such things deserve to die, they not only do them but approve those who practice them."* (Rom.1:19-32).

Man's proper response to the revelation of God should have been worship and grateful acknowledgment:

> *"For even though they knew God, they did not honour Him as God, or give thanks …"*

Man's response to natural revelation is three-fold. First of all is the initial act of rejection: Men simply refuse to accept God as He has revealed Himself. Paul tells us in verse 18 that men

> *"… suppress the truth in unrighteousness."*

They refuse God as He is. How often we consider the problem of the heathen to be lack of revelation. We somehow view God as withholding revelation essential to the salvation of the pagan. But Paul describes the heathen as having confined God's revelation to a box of their own making, and piling on the lid of the box their own sins. The pagan's problem is not the sparsity of revelation, but the suppression of it.

Whenever we reject one explanation of the facts we must necessarily counter with an alternative. This is precisely the situation with the heathen. They have rejected God's revelation of Himself and they have replaced it with another. The key word here is '*exchanged*' (vv. 23, 25, 26). Instead of worshipping the God Who made man in His own image, they made gods in their image. They worshipped the creature rather than the Creator. It is bad enough to conceive of God in terms of humanity, but they went far beyond this to represent God in terms of the beasts of the earth. The Greeks had their Apollo, the Romans the eagle, the Egyptians the bull, and the Assyrians the serpent. Paul may have been alluding to these 'gods.'

Not only did the heathen exchange the truth of God for a lie, but they also exchanged the blessings of God in His provision for sexual fulfilment for that which is unnatural and disgusting.

> "... *for their women exchanged the natural function for that which is unnatural, and in the same way also the men abandoned the natural function of the woman and burned in their desire towards one another ...*"

We may see here, a deadly sequence of events. Rejection of God's revelation leads to idolatry, and idolatry leads to immorality, and man at last plummets into the grossest perversions imaginable. Is this not our present experience in what I firmly believe are the end-times?

If you have thought of the heathen as an idolater because he didn't know any better, Paul insists that he is an idolater because he has refused to know better, suppressing God's self-revelation. As such, he has no excuse!

But the born-again disciple of Jesus; the adopted child of God the Father; the living temple of God the Holy Spirit; will be clothed in the very righteousness of the Lord Jesus. And we will have something to say – simply: "I am His and He is mine." And He, our heavenly Advocate, will gladly affirm that claim.

And then this love; this agapē love; this love of God implanted in my heart, will affect my attitude towards my fellow-man.

Because I will be more loving towards my fellows, not in an emotional sense, but in an evaluational sense. I will put a greater value on others; I will treat them as God would have me treat them – whether I find them particularly likeable, or not.

> *"If any one says, 'I love God,' and hates his brother, he is a liar; for he who does not love his brother whom he has seen, cannot love God Whom he has not seen. And this commandment we have from Him, that he who loves God should love his brother also."* (vs.20-21).

There are some who claim to be Christian of whom it may well be said that they are too heavenly-minded to be of any earthly use! But John is not in that group. He is, whilst able to soar to amazing heights of spirituality, still able to be intensely practical. And so he reminds his readers – including you and me – that God's own command is to love one another, that His love might be seen in us.

The challenge that comes to the child of God, is that (s)he love even as Father God loved, and continues to love. Is that how you and I love? If it is, then we may praise God for the fact. If it is not – at least not in the measure that we now know is expected of us – then we must seek His help; if necessary, seek His new birth; and be found, abiding in Him, and He in us, that His love might be perfected in us.

Chapter 12.

The three tests, and the new life.

In this chapter of the book, we move into the closing chapter of this 1st Letter from John and, as we do so, we are immediately confronted with all three of the tests that John has set before us, time and time again, throughout the earlier part of the letter.

> *"Every one who believes that Jesus is the Christ, is a child of God, and every one who loves the parent loves the child. By this we know that we love the children of God, when we love God and obey His commandments."* (vs 1-2)

Belief; love; obedience – the tests by which I may know that I am truly a child of Father God; born-again of God the Holy Spirit; a joint-heir with the Lord Jesus, the Christ.

The main emphasis, however, in this last chapter, is on life – the new life that the disciple of Jesus has received from the Father; the new life that I received when I was born-again of the Spirit, and in which faith, and love, and obedience may grow and flourish. We look, first of all, at the faith that procures this new life.

The great Dr Thomas Chalmers is reported as having described faith as being like the empty hand of a beggar that receives a gift while adding nothing to it. And that's just about it! Father God requires that I have faith in order to receive this new life – but even the faith is the gift, of God.

John speaks of what God would give.

> "… *this is the testimony, that God gave us eternal life, and this life is in His Son.*" (v.11).

Here we have the new life described – it is "eternal life", and that doesn't have to do with the length of it, in the sense of time, because eternity is not time, although it encompasses time, but with the quality of it. It is the life of God Himself; the best life; the only real life! And it isn't just for the future – "pie in the sky when you die"; it is something that the genuine disciple of Jesus experiences, and enjoys, even now. As a born-again child of God, I already possess eternal life!

Certain things are involved in this: new relationships for one. I have a new relationship with Almighty God – I can truly call Him my heavenly Father in a relationship of love that makes obedience to Him not an obligation, or a burden, but a joy and a delight. And I have a new relationship with my brothers and sisters in Jesus. We are, as Paul wrote to the Galatian believers, and as the annual Keswick Convention has as its motto,

> "... *all one in Christ Jesus.*" (Gal.3:28).

I even have a new relationship with unbelievers – seeing them, now, as individuals for whom Jesus also died, and I want to lead them to Him by prayer; by example; by direct witnessing.

Of course, this isn't always easy! And nowhere in the Scriptures have I ever found any suggestion that it would be – rather, it is the very opposite that is warned about! But, praise God, the new life also brings new resources.

> "*I can do all things*" wrote Paul, "*through Christ Who strengthens me.*" (Phil.4:13).

This new life is the very life of Jesus; divine life; and in it, and in Him, are all of the power and resources that I need.

But, as I said at the beginning, before I can receive what God would give, there is something that I must have.

And that is faith – faith in the Lord Jesus, the Christ. John uses the word "believe" –

> "*Every one who believes that Jesus is the Christ is a child of God, …*" (v.1)

but, of course, in this context, 'faith' and 'belief' are synonymous. Indeed, the same Greek word – πιστευο (pisteuo) – is translated by both. Of course, this faith, or belief, in the Lord Jesus means much more than simply believing that He exists and that He walked this earth some 2,000 years ago. After all, as James reminds us, in that sense of the word:

> *"Even the demons believe—and shudder."* (2:19).

It is not just believing that He hung on a cross and died. That is only what someone has termed "an intellectual assent to the truth of an historical fact."!

So what does it mean to believe that Jesus is the Christ, the Messiah of God? Well, what we are speaking of here is not faith in the fact that the Christ died, but faith/trust in the Christ Who died; a faith that is prepared to take whatever He gives, and to trust Him, in obedience whatever He may ask.

Faith in the Saviour is akin to that which I place in a surgeon to whom I commit my life on an operating table. It is a blend of dependence upon, and obedience to, another in whom I have complete confidence, knowing him to be what he is, and who he is.

And that is the faith that procures this new life that Father God longs to give. However, while you and I may have this faith that procures this new life, we must be aware of the foes who resent this new life.

You see, when we become possessors of this new life, we find that there is a line of demarcation drawn between those who possess it, and those who don't. John explains the distinction clearly and succinctly:

> "*He who has the Son has life; he who has not the Son of God, has not life.*"

No need for long, theological discourse and discussion there! No possibility of sitting on the fence! No 'hopes', 'maybes', or 'trying to's! Mankind is divided into two camps – believers and unbelievers; those who have this new life, and know it; and those who don't have it. As we walk the way of the disciple of Jesus – and remember that, at the beginning His disciples were known as "the people of the Way" – we find that there is a hostility that we meet.

Three times in vs 4-5, John uses the phrase

> "*overcomes the world*",

and the reason why the disciple of Jesus needs to overcome the world is that the world wants to overcome the disciple of Jesus! But why should this be? Simply because the world resents the fact that the disciple of Jesus has responded to the truth of Almighty God; responded in a way in which the unbeliever lacks either the courage, or the desire, to respond. And the response of the disciple condemns and reproves the failure of the world.

In John 17 we have the real Lord's Prayer and in it He prays, concerning His disciples,

> "*I have given them Thy word;* **and the world has hated them because they are not *of* the world**, *even as I am not of the world.*" (17:14; *emphasis added*).

This is one reason why it is so terribly sad when a well-known figure, who claims to be a true disciple of Jesus, speaks, or acts, in a manner that is unworthy of the Gospel. Such a person gives the world some ready ammunition. "You're no different to us"! Even worse, that person loses their own testimony, and will find it increasingly difficult to witness to the saving and renewing power of Jesus the Christ.

The basic difference between the disciple of Jesus and the unbeliever is not how "nice" they are, but in their attitude to, and acceptance of, the Lord Jesus. It is, sadly, sometimes true that a non-believer appears to be living a better life than the professed disciple, but this is not the main criterion by which we are judged. Jesus, Himself – as we have already noted – provides that criterion when He asks some Pharisees:

"What do you think of the Christ?" (Mt.22:42).

I think that it is C.S.Lewis who, in one of his books, makes the point that if we are to judge on the basis of how good, or nice, we find a person to be, we shouldn't compare disciple A with non-believer B and say that B is a better person. Rather, we should compare A with what he was before he became a disciple of Jesus; and B with what he might be if he were to become a disciple of Jesus!

But we may be assured that possession of the new life in Jesus will provide a reaction on the part of the world – certainly, the persecuted church in more than sixty countries, will testify to that! Such hostility may be expressed in different ways; the pressures may come from various directions; but it will be there – and we will be aware of it. Someone has said that "a Christian is rather like somebody who, until his conversion, has been drifting with the tide; and then suddenly decides to swim against it."

But, praise the Lord, this isn't the whole story. Because the hostility that we meet is more than matched by the ability we have.

And this, of course, ties in with the resources of which we thought earlier. In v.4, John writes:

> "... *whatever is born of God overcomes the world;*"

He uses the neuter "whatever" in order to emphasise, not the victorious person, but the victorious power. It is not the man, but his new birth and all that that entails, that overcomes. It is the very divine nature, that dwells within the believer, that conquers. Now, the person **is** victorious – Paul writes to his friends in Rome:

> "... *in all these things we are more than conquerors through Him Who loved us.*" (Rom.8:37).

But it is the power that the disciple has received that brings the victory.

> "*He Who is in you is greater than he who is in the world.*"

John has already assured us (4:4) and if we are in Jesus, and He is in us, then we have ability that can handle any hostility – even unto death, as so many in the persecuted church know!

And, of course, the link between the disciple and this power, is his faith; a faith that becomes stronger and more confident with experience as it proves, time and time again, that Jesus is right, and that the world is wrong.

So John speaks of the faith that procures new life; he warns against the foes who resent this new life; and then he deals with the facts that confirm this new life.

One of the things that we have already noted, on more than one occasion, is John's pastoral heart as he offers a word of encouragement to his readers. And, in this section of the letter, we find him doing so yet again. He is concerned here with the objective evidence, that is to say, with the confirmation that I may have, concerning this new life; confirmation that comes from outside of myself. And so he writes:

> *"This is He Who came by water and blood, Jesus Christ, not with the water only but with the water and the blood."* (v.6).

His reference to *"water"* speaks of the baptism of the Lord Jesus; and *"blood"* speaks of His crucifixion.

The baptism of Jesus, we have already learned, has to do with the message of His total identification with mankind; while His death on the cross has to do with the message of reconciliation to God, through that atoning sacrifice.

John gives us this wonderful assurance that, at the heart of the experience of the disciple of Jesus, lies a series of historical events; the declared and accomplished purpose of Almighty God recorded in that which took place, and to which nothing can ever be added, or from which nothing can ever be taken away. My faith rests, not merely in any feeling or emotion that I may have – because feelings and emotions can so easily change; not even on anything that Jesus said, on its own; but also on what He did. At the foundation of the true Christian experience is a Person; and not only a Person but also a purpose – a purpose that has been completely fulfilled in that Person.

The objective evidence – it doesn't depend on me; and for that, I am infinitely grateful! But there is also the subjective evidence. That is to say, the evidence from within. John, in v.8, adds another witness to the water and the blood. He writes:

> *"There are three witnesses, the Spirit, the water, and the blood; and these three agree."*

This is, of course, a reference to the inner conviction that is a gift of God the Holy Spirit, and a hallmark of a true conversion experience.

A disciple of Jesus; when speaking of his faith, doesn't use expressions such as "I think that I'm a disciple of Jesus", or "I hope that I'm a disciple of Jesus", or "I'm trying to be a disciple of Jesus". A true, born-again, Bible-believing, disciple of Jesus knows that he is so!

Reginald White, a former Principal of the Baptist Theological College in Glasgow, writes in one of his books: "In the last resort, a man knows the Gospel is true by his experience of its power within himself; and only the original, apostolic message about Jesus has that saving efficacy."

The life on which fellowship is based. Do you have that life? And if not, why not? It's freely offered to you – and all that you need do is to accept it, by faith. If you do, you'll meet those who will resent how you then live; but you'll be surrounded, and filled, with factual confirmation of what you then know; and all to the greatest possible end – even the praise and glory of Almighty God.

Chapter 13

Assurance!

With this chapter, we thunder around the last bend before entering the home straight, with the finishing line as our goal! In this chapter, we take our penultimate look at the First Letter from John, the beloved disciple and apostle.

In doing so, we find ourselves returning to what Eric Alexander – whose Bible Readings, in this letter at the Keswick Convention of 1976, you will recall, engendered my interest in this particular book of the New Testament – referred to as "the great purpose of the letter", namely 'assurance'.

Some days before I was inducted as minister of Bellshill: St. Andrew's Parish Church, I met an old friend who, I discovered, had moved to that area. He had heard that St Andrew's had called a new minister, and was delighted that it should be someone whom he already knew. As we talked about the town, and the congregation, he informed me: "You'll discover that you have many born-again believers in your congregation. The trouble is that they don't know it!"

That, I would suggest, is why so many need assurance. And it may be that there is someone reading these words who, in spite of the façade that they present, still don't have that assurance of the fullness of their salvation.

John opens this final section:

> "*I write this to you who believe in the name of the Son of God, that you may **know** that you have eternal life.*"

The NEB translates that verse:

> "*This letter is addressed **to assure you** that you have eternal life. It is addressed to those who give their allegiance to the Son of God.*"

In the previous chapter we were dealing, basically, with the new life that is offered to us in Christ Jesus, and the acceptance we must make of it. In this chapter, we are still concerned with that new life, but now we must look at the assurance that we may have of it. John wrote his account of the Gospel record, we read,

> "*… that you may believe that Jesus is the Christ, the Son of God, and that believing you may have life in His Name.*" (20:30).

That is to say, he set down the Gospel record in order that sinners might be brought to a knowledge, and experience, of salvation. However, when he penned this letter, he was writing to those who had experienced that salvation, that they might have that full assurance that is the sequel to faith.

We need to be reminded, often for our own encouragement, that salvation and assurance are not the same thing. Have you received, and appropriated, the new life that He offers? Then you may look to Him again, for assurance; positively, and actively, taking Him at His word. As you do, you will find that your faith is freed from any burden of doubt.

I use the word "burden" quite deliberately, because doubt and uncertainty are never easy things to bear. They press down heavily on our spirits; they make us unhappy; they leave us bewildered. And I would venture to claim that the doubts that cause the greatest misery are in the realm of personal relationships – uncertainty about how another person feels towards us. How terrible it must be to be left, merely wondering if someone loves me! In spite of our frequent joking, my wife and I have a wonderful, and satisfying, relationship. And our happiness comes, to a great extent, in the certain knowledge that we have that we love one another, and do so deeply. We just don't doubt it. If we ever were to do so, then I have no doubt that such a time of uncertainty would be a miserable time.

This applies also to uncertainty about our relationship with Almighty God – and if we have doubts there, that can be the most depressing and upsetting situation of all. Of course, there is a presumption of which faith may be accused.

There are those who claim that it is presumptuous of anyone to claim that they are sure of their salvation; to say, with absolute conviction, "Yes, I am a disciple of Jesus; I am saved, by grace, through faith in Him." Rev. George B. Duncan would tell of a friend from the Isle of Skye who, if asked, "Are you a Christian?" would never venture beyond "I'll be hoping so." He felt that it would be almost boasting to say anything more. But assurance is not boasting of my own achievements – I know, only too well, that there is nothing of which I could boast. It is relying on the grace of Almighty God.

Let me illustrate, again, from the marriage relationship. If I am asked "Are you married?", no-one thinks it presumptuous of me to answer, quite emphatically: "Yes". Indeed, I would be looked at a little strangely if my reply was to be: "I hope so"; or "I think so"; or "I'm doing my best to be"; or "It's not really for me to say." Because, of course, I'm not being asked to declare that I am the best husband who has ever lived; or even that I am a good husband. I am merely being asked, "Are you in this relationship?"

Was Paul being presumptuous when he wrote to young Timothy:

> "… *I am not ashamed, for I know the One in Whom I have put my trust, and **I am sure** that He is able to guard until that day what I have entrusted to Him.*"
> (II Tim.1:12; NRSV; *emphasis added*)?

Or was he being presumptuous when he wrote to the early believers living in Rome:

> "... *in all these things we are more than conquerors through him who loved us. For **I am sure** that neither death, nor life, nor angels, nor principalities, nor things present, nor things to come, nor powers, nor height, nor depth, nor anything else in all creation, will be able to separate us from the love of God in Christ Jesus our Lord.*" (8:37-39)?

So this accusation of presumption, if I assert that I am saved, does not stand. Indeed, if I have accepted, and am living, the new life in Christ Jesus, then it would be presumptuous to fail to take Him at His word; to doubt His own promises! One commentator (not identified in my original notes!) writes: "The assurance of which John is writing here, has no hint of pride or presumption about it. John is not thinking in terms of conceit or self-confidence; of self-righteousness. The assurance of which the Bible speaks has nothing in common with a presumptuous spirit."

At least part of the defence against this accusation of human presumption is God's intention.

If God is love, as John has earlier asserted then, surely, He is not going to foster uncertainty. Love always desires to end doubt! And God's Word shows that intention so clearly:

> "*I know Whom I have believed*"

writes Paul as we have already noted.

> "*We know that we have passed from death to life*"

writes John (I John 3:14), possibly quoting the words of Jesus Himself:

> "*Truly, truly, I say to you, he who hears My word and believes Him Who sent Me, **has** eternal life; he does not come into judgment, but has passed from death to life.*" (John 5:24; *emphasis added*).

The whole testimony of the New Testament is that Christians; disciples of Jesus; should know – that they should have assurance.

Have you come to Jesus in humility; in repentance; in sincerity; in truth? Have you opened your life wholly to Him? Then hold your head high, because you are one of the divine family; a child of the King! He has promised, and His Word is sure.

The second thing that we learn here is that our faith must rest on a basis of truth.

There isn't much point in the burden of doubt being lifted just now if I discover, later, that my freedom is based on a falsehood! So, what is truth? That is the question most famously asked by the Roman Procurator of Judaea, Pontius Pilate, when Jesus stood before him. (Jn.18:38). Of course, Jesus had already given the answer – even if Pilate had not been around to hear it. Thomas had asked Him,

> *"Lord, we do not know where You are going; how can we know the way?" Jesus said to him, "I am the way, and the truth, and the life; no one comes to the Father, but by me."* (Jn.14:5-6),

and John writes, here, to those

> *"… who believe in the Name of the Son of God, …"* (v.13).

So the truth on which my faith is based is Jesus – all that He is; all that He has done, and will do; all that He has said, and will say. It's the same glorious fact all over again – that the basis of my assurance is not in me at all; it's in Him!

There are a couple of aspects of the Person of the Lord Jesus that are closely related to the assurance that Father God means me to have concerning my salvation, the first of which concerns what He did.

That, of course, refers supremely to what He did on the cross at Calvary. In a mystery that is beyond all human understanding, God the Son, in His death, did something about the sin of the world; something that we could never have done; that He alone could do; and that never need be done again.

> *"For Christ also died for sins **once for all**, the righteous for the unrighteous, that He might bring us to God, being put to death in the flesh but made alive in the spirit;"*

writes Peter (I Pet.3:18; *emphasis added*). When I

"… *believe in the Name of the Son of God,* …"

it means that I am trusting One Who loved me and gave Himself for me.

"A wonderful Saviour is Jesus my Lord", begins one of the songs that I used to sing; while one of the grand old Gospel songs contains this amazing, astounding, affirmation:

"My sin – oh the bliss of this glorious thought! –
**my sin, not in part, but the whole
is nailed to His cross, and I bear it no more:**
Praise the Lord, praise the Lord, oh my soul." (Horatio G.Spafford; *emphasis added*).

Faith in what others do, and have done, is something that is common in our daily living – faith in the skill, and experience, and workmanship, of others – mostly complete strangers! In the spiritual realm, my faith reaches out to, and rests on, the very Son of God Who died that my sins might be forgiven, and Who knows me better than I know myself. That victorious shout: "*Tetelestai!*" – "Finished" – tells me that Jesus knew that He had completed the work of redemption and reconciliation; His being raised from the dead by the Father assures me that He has set His seal of approval upon the work of the Son. The work was perfectly done – nothing that I can do can add to it, or take away from it. Hallelujah!

My faith, then, rests in Christ Jesus: in what He did, and in what He said.

What a Bible Study that would be! Just to go through all of the promises that Jesus made; His statements; words that I may trust implicitly.

> *"Everyone the Father gives Me will come to Me, and whoever comes to Me I will certainly not turn away."* (Jn.6:37; CJB).

Have I come? Then I have been received! I have not been turned away!

Did He not say:

> *"Peace I leave with you; My peace I give to you; not as the world gives do I give to you. Let not your hearts be troubled, neither let them be afraid."*? (Jn.14:27).

Then why should I worry about anything? It was that fine son of Scotland, who ended up as Chaplain to the Senate of the United States of America, Rev. Dr. Peter Marshall, who said that "Ulcers are the badge of our unbelief"!

> *"Behold, I stand at the door and knock; if any one hears My voice and opens the door, I will come in to him and eat with him, and he with Me."* (Rev.3:20).

Remembering, of course, that these words were delivered to those who claimed to **be** His disciples, I may know that if I have heard His voice, and opened myself to Him afresh, that He will renew fellowship with me. Am I lukewarm in my faith and service? He still stands and waits, patiently, for me to realise that I am

> "… *wretched, pitiable, poor, blind, and naked.*" (v.17).

He is not impatient – the word used has the sense of "I have taken my stand". He desires to fellowship with us – as individuals! The Laodiceans were an independent church that thought that they had need of nothing; but they were not abiding in the Christ and drawing their power from Him. They had a 'successful programme', but it was not bearing the fruit that comes from abiding in Jesus. (see Jn.15:1-8).

If Jesus is the Person I believe Him to be, then His word is sufficient for me!

Faith in what **He** did; faith in what **He** said. Here is the basis on which my faith will rest.

The burden from which my faith is freed; the basis on which my faith must rest; and then John goes on to speak of the blessings to which my faith will lead.

Blessings that come because of the new relationship that I have with Father God, through the atoning sacrifice of the Lord Jesus, and the indwelling presence of God the Holy Spirit.

John stresses two aspects of that relationship. There is, first of all the way that is open.

> "*We can approach God with confidence ...*"

is how the N.E.B. translators render the beginning of v.14. Assurance leads to confidence; and the confidence, here, is that

> "*if we ask anything that accords with His will, He hears us.*" (CJB).

> "*... that accords with His will ...*"

Prof Barclay writes: "Here indeed is something to ponder. We are so apt to think that prayer is asking God for what we want; whereas true prayer is asking God for what He wants ... In the last analysis, the only true prayer is the prayer that says 'Thy will be done', and whose only request is for grace to accept that will, and strength to do it." (*in loc.*). On my study wall is a home-made plaque that reads: "Sincere prayer is not an attempt to influence the Will of God; but a genuine desire to bring my will into line with His."

Does this mean that we no longer need to bring our intercessions before Him? By no means! Paul exhorts young Pastor Timothy:

> "*First of all, then, I urge that supplications, prayers, intercessions, and thanksgivings be made for all people, ...*" (I Tim.2:1; ESV).

James writes:

> "*Is anyone among you sick? Let him call for the elders of the church, and let them pray over him, anointing him with oil in the name of the Lord.*" (5:14; ESV).

In Acts 9, we read of Peter:

> "*Now there was at Joppa a disciple named Tabitha, which means Dorcas. She was full of good works and acts of charity. In those days she fell sick and died; and when they had washed her, they laid her in an upper room. Since Lydda was near Joppa, the disciples, hearing that Peter was there, sent two men to him entreating him, "Please come to us without delay." So Peter rose and went with them. And when he had come, they took him to the upper room. All the widows stood beside him weeping, and showing tunics and other garments, which Dorcas made while she was with them. But Peter put them all outside and knelt down and prayed; then turning to the body he said, "Tabitha, rise." And she opened her eyes, and when she saw Peter she sat up.*" (36-40).

It's all to do with "*His will*".

> "*if we ask anything that accords with His will, He hears us.*"

He, that is Father God, hears – He wants to hear; He is willing to hear; He is waiting to hear; He listens carefully. Us – insignificant little people; sinful, selfish, little people; but having been brought, through the Lord Jesus, the Christ, into an amazing and unique relationship with Father God. Through Him the way into Almighty God's most holy presence, has been opened. When He died on the cross, we read that the veil of the Temple – that visible curtain that symbolised the fact that man's sin cut him off from his Creator – that veil was torn in two, from top to bottom, as if the very hand of God had reached down to rip it; and the way was opened. And, according to the anonymous writer of the Letter to Hebrew disciples of Jesus, we now

> "... *have confidence to enter the sanctuary by the blood of Jesus, by the new and living way which He opened for us through the curtain, that is, through His flesh, ...*" (10:19-20).

And then John stresses the fact that answers are certain.

> "*And if we know that He hears us is whatever we ask, we know that we have obtained the requests made of Him.*"

If I ask in accordance with His will, then my request will be granted – the answer to my prayer will be "Yes"! That is what has happened when people say "My prayer was answered"! But every prayer is answered. And if the answer happens to be "No", or "Wait", then I must question either the request, or its timing. But please, never say that God doesn't answer, or didn't answer, your prayers. Answers are certain.

Before we finish this chapter, we must also look at vs 16-17 – a short passage that some may have difficulty in understanding. Prof. Barclay heads his commentary on these two verses with the words: "Praying for the brother who sins". And this, of course, is the primary lesson that the passage contains. "It is an urgent appeal to pray for an erring brother – or sister! – rather than gossip, or be censorious about them." (*in loc.*).

Colin Kruse suggests that: "A better approach is to examine who it is, in I John, that the author sees committing sins which do, and do not, lead to death. It is the 'brother' whose sin is not unto death for whom the readers are urged to pray. This suggests that the sin that does not lead to death is most likely that of the believer. If this is the case, then the sin that does lead to death is most likely that of the unbeliever. Within the overall context of I John, where the secessionists are now regarded as unbelievers, even antichrists, the sin that leads to death is probably the sin of the secessionists, in particular their denial that Jesus is the Christ come in the flesh, and that His death is necessary for salvation." (*The Letters of John*; Eerdmans, Grand Rapids, 2000; p.194).

The mortal, or deadly, sin to which John refers, is the sin that brings eternal death, i.e. separation, for eternity, from Father God. And what is this terrible sin? Jesus said:

> "... *no sin, no slander, is beyond forgiveness for men, except slander spoken against the Spirit, and that will not be forgiven ... ... if anyone speaks against the Holy Spirit, for him there is no forgiveness, either in this age, or in the age to come.*" (Mt.12:31; NEB).

And this sin against the Holy Spirit is not one isolated act; it is a persistent and deliberate rejection of the truth; a progressive hardening of the heart; that leads to a state in which a person is, literally, past praying for! What a state to be in! But the warning is there, and there can be no excuse.

David Jackman, in *The message of John's letters* (IVP, Leicester, 1988) writes: "... the sin that leads to death does so because, by its very nature, it rejects the only means by which sin may be forgiven – the atoning death of the incarnate Son of God. This underlines the important truth that it is not this sin that is *unpardonable*, but that it *remains unpardoned*. ... Purification from *every* sin has already been assured through 'the blood of Jesus', so Christians are those whose sins (all of them) have been forgiven (2:12). Yet no believer in Christ can reckon himself sinless, or imagine that he can dispense with a continuing forgiveness (1:8), so we need constantly to confess our sins and to call upon Christ for pardon and purification from *all* unrighteousness (1:9).

The sin that leads to death is unforgiven and remains unforgiven because it refuses to appropriate the gracious means of pardon which God has provided. 'Death is its natural, but not its absolutely inevitable, consequence. It is possible to close the heart against the influences of God's Spirit so obstinately and persistently that repentance becomes a moral impossibility. Just as the body may starve itself to such an extent as to make the digestion, or even the reception, of food impossible; so the soul may go on refusing offers of grace until the very power to receive grace perishes.' (A.Plummer, The Epistles of St John; CUP, 1894)" (pps 164-5).

However, "If you're worried that you may be guilty of the unforgivable sin, you almost certainly are not," Rick Cornish aptly points out in his book, *Five Minute Theologian*. "Concern about committing it reveals the opposite attitude of what the sin is. Those who might be guilty wouldn't care because they have no distress or remorse over the possibility."

Note, too, that those words were spoken by the Lord Jesus, not to His disciples, or to the people in general, but specifically to Pharisees who had personally witnessed His miracle of completely and instantly healing a blind and mute demon-possessed man (see Mt.12:22). Rather than acknowledging the obvious fact that Jesus was exercising divine powers, the Pharisees were so spiritually depraved that they attributed His power to Satan (v. 24).

"Their problem was not blind ignorance, but wilful rejection," points out Cornish. "That deliberate refusal to believe, even though knowing the truth, seems to be what Jesus called the unforgivable sin."

"... while the child of God is capable of sin, but not marked by it ... the essential characteristic of those who are not born of God is that they are sinful, but do not acknowledge this (1:8, 10)." (Stephen S.Smalley, *1,2,3 John (World Biblical Commentary)*; Word (UK) Ltd, Milton Keynes, 1984; pps 99-100)

Assurance! Do you have it? Has your faith been freed from doubt? Is it based on Him Who **is** Truth? Then it will lead to all the blessings that Father God waits to pour out upon you; and you will be used to draw others back to Him.

What an amazing life this is! The tragedy is that so many fail to experience it, or value it, as God intended us to. May He grant that this is **not** the case, for you or for me.

Chapter 14

The disciple's experience.

In this, our final look at John's first letter, we come to what has been referred to as "the three triumphant certainties" with which the apostle ends his letter, and each of which is introduced with the words "*we know*". Here are no tentative, hesitant, suggestions," writes John Stott, "but bold, dogmatic, Christian affirmations which are beyond all dispute, and which neatly summarise truths already introduced in earlier parts of the Epistle." (*in loc.*).

> "*I write this to you who believe in the Name of the Son of God, that you may know that you have eternal life. And this is the confidence which we have in Him, that if we ask anything according to His will He hears us. And if we know that He hears us in whatever we ask, we know that we have obtained the requests made of Him. If any one sees his brother committing what is not a mortal sin, he*

> *will ask, and God will give him life for those whose sin is not* mortal. *There is sin which is mortal; I do not say that one is to pray for that. All wrongdoing is sin, but there is sin which is not mortal. We know that any one born of God does not sin, but He who was born of God keeps him, and the evil one does not touch him. We know that we are of God, and the whole world is in the power of the evil one.*
>
> *And we know that the Son of God has come and has given us understanding, to know Him Who is true; and we are in Him Who is true, in His Son Jesus Christ. This is the true God and eternal life. Little children, keep yourselves from idols."*

The first certainty of which John speaks centres around what we may describe as the security of the experience of the disciple of Jesus.

This is, of course, the assurance of which we have been thinking, time and time again, but seen from another specific perspective. John reminds his readers of that perfection to which the disciple of Jesus will aspire:

> *"We know that anyone born of God does not sin …"*

This is the same statement that John has already made, and we have already noted that he is not suggesting some doctrine of so-called "sinless perfection"; that the born-again believer, the child of the living God, never sins. His use of the tense in the Greek language that is named the present continuous is, of course, the key. So what he is actually saying is that to those who, by the new birth, are now the possessors of the Divine nature, sin is no longer the pleasurable, natural, desirable thing to do; that what used to be enjoyed is enjoyed no longer. He is writing, here, of the persistent, continual, indulgence in sin that is no longer contemplated by the believer. You may remember the illustration that I used earlier in the book. If a pig and a sheep were both to fall into a muddy pool, the sheep would struggle to get out, while the pig would wallow, quite contentedly, in the mud. Both are prone to fall – but the differences in their natures brings about a difference in their reactions!

One commentator, quoted by Prof. Barclay, says: "A child of God may sin, but his normal condition is resistance to evil." And someone else has said that "a saint is not a man who never falls; he is a man who gets up and goes on, every time he does fall." We might add, of course, that he does so by the grace of God.

This is why, every day, when I have confessed my sins, and claimed the forgiveness that has been gained for me, at the cost of His own blood, by the Lord Jesus, I go on to ask that the Lord would continue to sanctify me, by the Spirit, through the blood, making me a little bit more like Jesus.

So the disciple of Jesus aims high; he aspires to perfection, even 'though he knows that, in this life, he will never attain it. But is it not the aspiration itself that keeps many away from the Christ? Is there a fear that they will be unable to attain the standard?

I consciously offered my life to the Lord a few days before I reached 15 years of age. In the Presbyterian tradition in which I had been raised, my next step should have been to attend the Communicants' Class – a class that prepared one for full membership of the congregation, including partaking of the Lord's Supper. However, I had read a fair bit of the Bible, even by then, and I knew those words of Paul, in I Cor.11:28 –

> "*Let a man examine himself, …*".

When I did so, I found myself falling far short of the standard that I knew was expected of me!

It was many months later that one of the elders of the congregation came to speak to the Boys' Brigade Sunday morning Bible Class. It was a "Communion Sunday" and he had chosen (or been led!) to speak on those very words that had caused me so much difficulty. However, he pointed out that Paul didn't stop there! he continued:

> "*… and so eat of the bread and drink of the cup.*"

The elder pointed out that the examination was not to keep us away from the Table, but to ensure that we approached it in the correct way – fully aware that, of ourselves, we have no right to come, but that we are commanded to come, and to do so by His grace!

What a relief to this young lad! There is a standard; and I shall never, in this mortal life, attain it. But His grace covers all, and so I may come and eat, and drink, and enjoy His presence. So many years later, I often make the point that the moment I decide that I am worthy, is the moment I make myself **un**worthy!

I recall a young couple coming to see me about being married. I explained to them that I did not perform "church weddings", but offered a Christian marriage service that was, indeed (in those days), normally conducted within the church building. They were happy with that, so I went on and spent more time explaining the ideals of Christian marriage, and of real Christianity. We then arranged to meet again, on the following week. That meeting never took place. A couple of days later I received a 'phone call from the girl's mother! "They've decided to make other arrangements." she said. "Your standards are too high"! Well, I did manage to inform her, before she hung up, that they were not my standards, but God's; I merely applied them. However, I was never able to explain to those two young people that there was another stage. For, of course, there is, as John reminds us, the protection of which the disciple of Jesus is assured.

"We know that anyone born of God does not sin."

And how do we know? Because

"He Who is the only-begotten of the Father keeps him, and the evil one does not touch him."

What a difference this makes to the whole situation! Not that the disciple of Jesus has to keep himself, but that he is kept!

Remember the opening salutation of Jude in his short letter. It was written

> "*To those who are called, beloved in God the Father and **kept** for Jesus Christ:*" (v.1; *emphasis added*).

J.B.Phillips translates:

> "*… to those who have obeyed the call, who are loved by God the Father and **kept** in the faith by Jesus Christ.*" (*emphasis added*).

Another translation in my notes (but without any reference!) states

> "*… those whom God has called, who live in the love of God the Father, and **in the safe-keeping** of Jesus, the Christ.*" (*emphasis added*).

What a tremendous truth this is – that the One Who saved us by His death will keep us by His power!

The story is told of an old slave who was being taunted about his recent conversion. "So,", said his tormentor, "you now have mastery over the devil?" "No," replied the old slave, "I ain't got mastery **ober** de devil; but I've got the Master **ob** de devil!"

And, of course, that's it. And, having Him, I am kept by His power. Remember John's words a little earlier:

> *"Little children, you are of God, and have overcome them; for He who is in you is greater than he who is in the world."* (4:4).

In my experience as a disciple of Jesus, I have this wonderful security, in Him.

John then makes his second affirmation as he writes: "We know that we are of God ..." And here, surely, his thinking is centred on the identity of the experience of the disciple of Jesus. This has to do with the source from which the disciple's life is derived.

"We know that we are of God ..."

The Greek, here, reads literally *"out of God"*. Just as a stream flowing out of a spring derives its waters form the spring, so the life of the disciple of Jesus is derived from the very heart of Father God, Himself. And this, of course, is why there is a wonderful unity between all those who have been truly born again of Holy Spirit – regardless of their denominational label, or lack thereof; their social status; their political persuasion. All are sharers in, and partakers of, the same life, derived from the same source. And this is also why there is such a close affinity between the believer and his Lord – as His disciple, I am united also with Him! There is a wonderful sense of "oneness" of mind and outlook; of thought and aspiration; between the disciple of Jesus and his Master.

> "*We know that we are of God ...*"

– what a tremendous assertion to be able to make. But John makes it; and all of those who have accepted the new life offered in, and through, the Lord Jesus – and available only in and through Him – can make it. It is an absolute certainty. And, because of it, John can also write of the sphere from which the disciple's life is released.

That sphere is, not surprisingly, the world and the power that rules over it.

> "*We know that we are children of God, and that the whole world lies in the power of the evil one.*" (v.19; Weymouth New Testament).

John Stott, to whom I have referred previously, emphasises John's use of the word "lies" (not as in "untruths"!). He writes: "It (the world) is not represented as struggling actively to be free, but as quietly lying, perhaps even unconsciously asleep, in the arms of satan."

Here is that truth, stated again and again in the pages of the New Testament, that if a person is not a disciple of Jesus, then his/her life is under the authority, power, and control of the enemy – and all of the rituals in the world won't make any difference!

> "*He who is not with Me,*"

said Jesus,

> "*is against Me.*" (Mt.12:30).

That's the choice – for or against; no "don't knows". This isn't a political poll to try to predict the outcome of an election. Listen, again, to John Stott: "John wastes no words and blurs no issue. The uncompromising alternative is stated baldly. Everyone belongs either to "us" or to "the world". There is no third category. Nowadays (and he was writing over 50 years ago!) when the line of demarcation between Church and world is confused, it is important to learn again that all but those who have had a heavenly birth are under the power of "… the world rulers of this present darkness …" (Eph.6:12), and of their chief, the god and prince of this world."

As you may have realised I often, like Paul, use marriage as an illustration of the life of the true disciple of Jesus. In terms of marriage, the world is divided into two 'camps' – those who are married, and those who are not. And the difference between them is that those who are married have entered into a particular, personal relationship with another human being. And, if I am not married, then that is how I become married! Similarly, I become a disciple of Jesus by entering into a particular, personal relationship with Him. But whereas my marital state has a limited effect on my life here and now, and no effect on my life hereafter; my relationship with Jesus, the Christ both effects my life now, and **determines** my life hereafter – whether it will be with the Saviour, or without Him yet knowing it to be my own fault and responsibility.

As a disciple of Jesus, I am released from the sphere of the world. The world's language, the world's standards, the world's values – all of these are things from which I have been released. There ought to be something unmistakeably different about the believer; something recognised by others, and immediately so by other believers. And it all comes from the identity of the experience of the disciple of Jesus.

John makes one further assertion in these closing verses. He has spoken of the security of the experience of the disciple of Jesus; of the identity of the experience of the disciple of Jesus; and now his thinking concerns the reality of the experience of the disciple of Jesus.

It was Karl Marx who claimed that "religion is the opiate of the masses"; in other words, he viewed religion as a kind of drug that gives one a temporary feeling of elation that takes one away from reality. Some years ago, I was asked to write an article for a German Christian magazine (the article was in English!) on the subject of reality. While I was preparing it, I asked one of my 16-year-old pupils what he understood by the term. His reply was "It's the opposite of being fake; it is something that is genuine; something real." That's not a bad definition. Marx' inference appears to have been that religion is all an illusion, an hallucination, like the state induced by a drug like opium.

But there is nothing phoney, or illusory, about the experience of the disciple of Jesus. And John, in v.20, speaks of two aspects of this reality. First of all, he refers to the historic reality

> "*We know that the Son of God has come ...*"

One of the books on my bookshelves is entitled "Evidence that demands a verdict", by Josh McDowall. It is a book of Christian Apologetics, i.e. a book that, as it were, sets out the case for the Christ, and for Christianity. The author points out that "... the writers of the N.T. wrote either as eyewitnesses of the events they described, or recorded eyewitness, first-hand, accounts of the events." He then quotes from Peter's second letter:

> "*For we did not follow cleverly devised tales when we made known to you the power and coming of our Lord Jesus Christ, but we were eyewitnesses of His majesty.*" (1:16; NASB),

and comments: "They certainly knew the difference between myth, legend, and reality. A professor of a "World Literature" class in which I was speaking asked the question, 'What do you think of Greek mythology?' I answered with another question: 'Do you mean were the events of the life of Jesus, the resurrection, virgin birth [better 'conception'!], etc. just myth?' He said, 'Yes'. I replied that there is one obvious difference between these things applied to Christ, and these things applied to Greek mythology, that is usually overlooked. The similar events, such as resurrection, etc., of

Greek mythology were not applied to real, flesh and blood, individuals but, rather, to [characters who were, themselves, mythological]. But when it comes to Christianity, these events are attached to a Person [Whom] the writers knew in time-space dimension history; the historic Jesus of Nazareth Whom they knew personally."

Now, there may well be some words and phrases there with which most of us are unfamiliar. But the basic thrust is clear: that there is an historical basis to my faith; that it rests on historical facts, historical events, historical and real people. In spite of the efforts of Greek philosophers, the basis of the Christian faith is not a philosophy of life that has been imagined, or thought out, or worked out, by man. It is something that has been revealed by, and carried through by, Almighty God. And how glad that should make us! Facts, not feelings (which may change like the breeze), are the foundation upon which my faith will rest.

But not only is there this historical reality; there is also a continual reality.

> "... *we know that the Son of God has come, and has given us understanding so that we may know Him Who is true;*"

John uses two different Greek words here, both of which are translated into English by "know". Some may be familiar with the similar situation in the French language with "savoir" – to know in a factual sense; and "connaître" – to know in a personal sense. The first word used by John indicates that I know something as a fact – "... *that the Son of God has come,*"; whilst the second has the sense of "to perceive and know in experience." So, through Jesus, I can come to a comprehension, an understanding, an intimate knowledge of God; and the tense used signifies a continuous and progressive comprehension.

The reality of the experience of the true disciple of Jesus – based on historical, verifiable, fact; and with a growing insight into the very mind of Almighty God, and a deepening experience of the wonderful grace of God. This is life as it was meant to be; this is

"... *life in all its fulness.*" (Jn.10:10);

this is 'Life with a capital L' (Lindsay Glegg).

John gives one last word of exhortation –

"*My children be on the watch against false gods.*"

In other words, keep yourselves from every counterfeit gospel; every misrepresentation and distortion; every exaggeration and substitute; that seeks to supplant the God and Father of our Lord Jesus, the Christ, as the object of your faith, devotion, and love. This is a timely word to the disciple of Jesus in the second decade of the third millennium. As I look at so much of the established church in the west, I see a constant dilution, distortion, and denial of the Gospel message – emanating, particularly, from many of those who are supposed to be its prime advocates!

Little children – and John uses again the tender and affectionate form of address that has not occurred since about half-way through the letter (3:18) – don't play with fire! I have described the fellowship – see that you don't let anything, or anyone, endanger it.

And what a wonderful fellowship it is – the fellowship of true disciples of Jesus, and their God. As we have looked at this great letter we have seen the light in which that fellowship is bathed; the love with which that fellowship is bound; the life on which that fellowship is based. May we also have been drawn closer, with deeper commitment, to the One Who sheds that light; Who shares that love; Who supplies that life - even "… *the true God* …", Father, Son, and Holy Spirit – to Whom be all glory, and honour, and praise, now, and throughout eternity.

II John and III John

Introduction

Although the original series of spoken messages, and the more recent teaching, were based solely on I John, it seems not inappropriate that, in this written form, we should look, briefly, at John's other letters.

These are the two shortest letters in the New Testament – indeed, it may be said that they are not as much letters, as brief notes, or memos. They are very personal letters, written to individuals, and one might wonder why God the Holy Spirit has had them preserved in the written Word of God. However, He has seen fit to do so, and we may therefore conclude that there are lessons contained within them that are of value to the Church in every age.

John Phillips comments: "We should certainly not make the mistake of underestimating their importance simply because they are brief. In the things of God, as we learn from the so-called "minor" prophets, it is a mistake to measure the man by the size of his manuscript; the Holy Spirit doesn't always inspire long books on order to convey vital beliefs. Weighty things can often be stated in a few dynamic words – "I love you", for instance, or "Don't touch", or "Exit", or "Help!"

We certainly don't expect a drowning man to express his urgent need in flowery paragraphs." (Phillips, *op.cit.*, p.211).

There are significant differences between the two letters. II John is written in a more formal manner, and to a community – albeit to an individual in that community. It is a warning against false teachers but, while majoring on doctrine, does not ignore the practicalities of the Christian faith.

III John is almost the opposite! It deals with the practicality of hospitality, but does not ignore doctrine. This reminds me of my own practice while pastoring the congregation of Bellshill: St Andrew's. In those far-off days, we had two diets of worship each Sunday. At the morning worship service, the building was well filled. This was when the 'nominal' members ensured that their names were kept on the Congregational Roll! I tended to preach on some topical subject – taken from current news, or from something mentioned/discussed when visiting my flock – as I presented the Gospel message. However, I always ensured that, in that message, there was an element of teaching!

In the evening, the reverse was the case. There – as with I John – I preached in a series, providing some teaching for those who were interested enough to make a second visit to the sanctuary. However, never knowing when an unbeliever might be there, I always sought to bring something of the basic Gospel message into that sermon.

So, in two appendices, let us look now at these two letters. Again, I do not propose to spend time on matters of authorship, date, and/or recipient. We shall take the Word, as it has been handed down to us, and seek to learn from that. We shall simply adopt the position that both letters were sent out by the apostle John, to some of those for whom he carried pastoral responsibility.

Appendix 1

II John

A warning against itinerant deceivers.

"The elder to the elect lady and her children, whom I love in the truth, and not only I but also all who know the truth, because of the truth which abides in us and will be with us for ever:

Grace, mercy, and peace will be with us, from God the Father and from Jesus Christ the Father's Son, in truth and love.

I rejoiced greatly to find some of your children following the truth, just as we have been commanded by the Father. And now I beg you, lady, not as though I were writing you a new commandment, but the one we have had from the beginning, that we love one another. And this is love, that we follow His commandments; this is the commandment, as you have heard from the beginning, that you follow love. For many deceivers have gone out into the world, men who will not acknowledge the coming of

Jesus Christ in the flesh; such a one is the deceiver and the antichrist. Look to yourselves, that you may not lose what you have worked for, but may win a full reward. Any one who goes ahead and does not abide in the doctrine of Christ does not have God; he who abides in the doctrine has both the Father and the Son. If any one comes to you and does not bring this doctrine, do not receive him into the house or give him any greeting; for he who greets him shares his wicked work.

Though I have much to write to you, I would rather not use paper and ink, but I hope to come to see you and talk with you face to face, so that our joy may be complete.

The children of your elect sister greet you."

The letter is addressed to

"… *the elect lady and her children,* …"

someone known to John, and to others, as a woman of truth, who is faithful to the Lord. I wonder how others think of me, and of you? Are we recognised as people of truth, faithful to the Lord Jesus, the Christ?! What is

> "... *the truth which abides in us and will be with us for ever:*"?

I would suggest that this is simply the truth of the Gospel message – summed up in those familiar words from John's account:

> "... *God so loved the world that He gave His only Son, that whoever believes in Him should not perish but have eternal life.*" (3:16).

What a wonderful word of commendation for this un-named sister! The lack of even a courtesy reference to her husband suggests that she was a widow, but that she was also a mother. As such, she had also been found faithful. So John can write:

> "*I rejoiced greatly to find some of your children following the truth, just as we have been commanded by the Father.*" (v.4).

Do these words imply that some of the lady's children were saved, and others not? I think that that is unlikely. What I suspect is that some had left home – as children do! – and without the modern means of communication, she would have been concerned that, away from her maternal influence, they may have strayed from the truth. What joy she would have experienced; what tears of joy she would have shed; when she received this brief note from the aged apostle assuring her that he had met with them, and that they were being found to be faithful!

I know that when I left my parental home for the first time, to enter the British Merchant Navy, this was one of the concerns of my own parents. However, although we had no internet with e-mails in those far-off days, I was at least able to make use of the postal services of the various countries I visited, to assure my parents that all was well!

Gooding makes the comment: "Let us, to whom God in His grace has given children pause with thankfulness and praise if God has, in His mercy, saved them; and in these wicked days let us, like Job, pray for them, ..." (Gooding, *op. cit.*, p.271). There can surely be no doubt that this dear lady had constantly upheld her own children in prayer, and that such prayer was, at least in part, instrumental in their faithfulness to the Lord.

Having commended both the elect lady, and her absent children, John moves on to a word of command.

> *"And now I beg you, lady, not as though I were writing you a new commandment, but the one we have had from the beginning, that we love one another. And this is love, that we follow His commandments; this is the commandment, as you have heard from the beginning, that you follow love."* (vs.5-6).

Just as he has pointed out in his first letter, John makes clear that this is no new commandment, but one which the elect lady and the church that may have met in her home, already knew. They are to express a mutual love, one for the other –

a love that is not the eroticism that was so common then, as it is now; not even familial love, or the love shared by close friends; but the highest form of love, *agapē*, the very love of Father God Himself. That love, John reminds her, is defined by following His commandments. And the commandments had already been summed up by the Lord Jesus:

> "… *when the Pharisees heard that He had silenced the Sadducees, they came together. And one of them, a lawyer, asked Him a question, to test Him. 'Teacher, which is the great commandment in the law?' And He said to him, 'You shall love the Lord your God with all your heart, and with all your soul, and with all your mind. This is the great and first commandment. And a second is like it, 'You shall love your neighbour as yourself.' On these two commandments depend all the law and the prophets.*" (Matt.22:34-40; *inter al*);

and, again:

> "*A new commandment I give to you, that you love one another; even as I have loved you, that you also love one another. By this all men will know that you are My disciples, if you have love for one another.*" (John 13:34-35).

"The only proof of our love of God is our love for the brethren" comments Prof. Barclay. But is it possible for someone to be commanded to love?! Yes, it is – but only if we are talking about *agapē* love which George Duncan often defined as "a minimum of emotion, and a maximum of evaluation." That means that Christian love, the love of which John writes, is fundamentally an act of the will. It is treating others as God has treated us – especially those

> "... *of the household of faith."* (Gal.6:10).

This, I would suggest, is the Biblical basis for the thought that it is possible to love someone whom we do not actually 'like'!

John then provides a word of caution to his friend. As in his first letter, he is concerned about those "wolves in sheep's clothing" who had infiltrated the church – and who are still to be found in her today!

> *"For many deceivers have gone out into the world, men who will not acknowledge the coming of Jesus Christ in the flesh; such a one is the deceiver and the antichrist."* (v.7).

Of course, there are still those who deny that Jesus was, and is, God; and those who would deny His humanity. John Stott comments: "He who denies the incarnation is not just *a deceiver and an antichrist*, but 'the deceiver and the antichrist' (RV, RSV) *par excellence.* 'the arch-deceiver' (NEB). There is in this heresy a double affront: it opposes Christ and deceives men. The false teachers were referred to in the First Epistle both as purposing to 'deceive' (ii.26. RSV) and as 'antichrists' (ii. 18, 22); now the two ideas are brought together." (op.cit. p.210)

However, there are many other forms of deception in the Church of the 21st century. There is the so-called 'prosperity gospel' that is no Gospel; there are those who claim that, for example, the Biblical injunctions against homosexuality (and I would submit that this word actually covers all forms of sexual deviancy and immorality) no longer apply because "we have moved on"! They either have never read; never understood; or deliberately ignore; words such as those of Paul:

> "***Do not be conformed*** *to this world but be transformed by the renewal of your mind, that you may prove what is the will of God, what is good and acceptable and perfect."* (Rom.12:2; *emphasis added*).

or of Peter:

> "*As obedient children, do **not be conformed** to the passions of your former ignorance, but as He who called you is holy, be holy yourselves in all your conduct;"* (I Peter 1:14-15; *emphasis added*).

Rather, they want the Church to conform to the society around about it. On the day on which I was typing these words, David Robertson published a blog post in which he made the following statement:

"The Christian church is largely in trouble because it ... has forsaken the living well of Christ for the broken cisterns of our culture - just see the numerous vicars in dog collars on everything from Come Dancing to Celebrity MasterChef -

who seem to have little, if any, acquaintance with the Christ they are supposed to follow and the Word they are supposed to preach."

John is quite clear that, regardless of how they may describe themselves, such people are servants of the evil one.

John draws this brief note to a close with a further warning regarding hospitality. Now, hospitality is something that is commended and, indeed, encouraged in Scripture. So Paul exhorts the Roman believers to:

> *"Contribute to the needs of the saints, practice hospitality."* (12:13);

while the writer of the letter to Hebrew disciples of Jesus states that they should

> *"... not neglect to show hospitality to strangers, for thereby some have entertained angels unawares."* (13:2);

and Peter tells his readers that they should

> *"Practice hospitality ungrudgingly to one another."* (I Peter 4:9).

However, John here instructs

> *"If any one comes to you and does not bring this doctrine, do not receive him into the house or give him any greeting;"* (v.10).

We must ask why this should be so – and John immediately provides the answer to our question:

> *"for he who greets him shares his wicked work."* (v.11).

The doctrine to which John refers is

> *"... the doctrine of Christ ..."* (v.9).

and he states that

> *"Anyone who goes ahead and does not abide in the doctrine ... does not have God;"* (v.9).

The significant words are "... *goes ahead* ...". These false teachers, like their equivalents today, would have us believe that they are the "progressives" while the church is static, and bogged down in the 19th century (if not earlier)! They come to us with their exciting innovations; their new style of 'worship' – that is, so often, mere entertainment; often their large buildings with all of the latest technology; their messages that are always sources of comfort and joy – but totally ignore anything that would suggest, or infer, that our God is a holy God Who, at the time of His choosing,

> *"... will judge the world in righteousness by a Man whom He has appointed, and of this He has given assurance to all men by raising Him from the dead."* (Acts 17:31).

This "progressive" theology is nothing of the sort! If it denies that Jesus, the Christ, has come in the flesh, then it is regressive. It is, in fact, calling Almighty God a liar. It is echoing the first recorded question to be asked on planet earth:

"Did God say …?" (Gen.3:1).

If we offer hospitality to those with this kind of teaching, then we are sharing in their evil, anti-Christ, work! Offering such false teachers hospitality is, effectively, saying that we accept their message; leaves us open to 'spiritual infection'; and provides such a person, or persons, with a validity based on what they may claim is their friendship with us, and our acceptance of them and their message.

"Of course, the church would be meeting in a house [perhaps the local church met in this lady's home]. To take the stranger in would, therefore, mean to accept his teaching and to welcome him into the fellowship of the church. To *welcome him* would similarly imply more than a formal politeness or recognition. It would be to express delight in his arrival, to foster friendship. But if that sort of behaviour is extended to false teachers, it is not so much Christian love as spiritual suicide. It does not show love to the rest of the flock, because it exposes them to heresy's insidious undermining of their faith. It does not even show love towards the deceiver, since it simply confirms him in his error, which he might now never be brought to admit. Above all, it does not express love for God, because it sides with evil in actively encouraging the spread of that which is most destructive of the truth." (Jackman, *op.cit.*, p.185).

How we need the gift of spiritual discernment – especially in these end-times!

However, we must also be careful not to go too far in the other direction! John is not saying that only those who have been born again by faith in the Lord Jesus, the Christ, should enter our homes! Only God knows how many have been brought into the Kingdom because of the friendship, and open door, of a neighbour, workmate, or family member.

F.F. Bruce comments: "The injunction not to receive anyone who does not bring 'the teaching of Christ' means that no such person must be accepted as a Christian teacher or as one entitled to the fellowship of the church. It does not mean that (say) one of J Ws ['Jehovah's Witnesses'] should not be invited into the house for a cup of tea in order to be shown the way of God more perfectly in the sitting-room than would be convenient on the doorstep.

But for a church, or its responsible leaders, knowingly to admit within its bounds the propagation of teaching subservice of the Gospel is to participate in what John describes as 'evil works'." (op.cit., p.142).

The conclusion of the letter makes a very important point – that face-to-face communication is superior to any written communication. This is, in fact, why some have difficulty with certain passages from the Word of God. I am thinking, for example, of the encounter that the Lord Jesus had with a certain Syrophoenician woman (Matt.15:21ff; Mark 7:24ff).

If we simply read the recorded words, we may end up with a picture of a Jesus Who is sharp, and unkind, in His response to this woman:

> "... *she begged Him to cast the demon out of her daughter. And He said to her, "Let the children first be fed, for it is not right to take the children's bread and throw it to the dogs."* (Mk.7:26-27).

However, if we can imagine that, as was almost certainly the case, there was a twinkle in the eyes of the Saviour as He spoke, and that there was a tone in His voice that cannot possibly be replicated in print, then we will surely come to a totally different conclusion! Indeed, I believe that it was that twinkle, and that tone, that encouraged her to respond as she did:

> "*But she answered Him, 'Yes, Lord; yet even the dogs under the table eat the children's crumbs'.*" (Mk.7:28).

It was such an answer that gladdened the heart of the Master, and led to the assurance He gave to her as

> *"... He said to her, "For this saying you may go your way; the demon has left your daughter." And she went home, and found the child lying in bed, and the demon gone."* (Mk.7:29-30).

Warren Wiersbe writes: "This little epistle written to a Christian mother and her children (and perhaps the church that met in their house), is a perfect gem of sacred correspondence. But we must not forget the major thrust of the letter: be alert! There are many deceivers in the world!" (*Be Alert*, a NT study; p.115).

The Church in these early years of the 21st century, and in what many believe to be the very end-times, needs to be as much on her guard against the deceivers who would seek to infiltrate her, as did the disciples of Jesus at the end of the 1st century. May God grant us the spiritual discernment to see through their deceit, and to live in the truth of the Gospel.

Appendix 2

III John

The spirit of control

"The elder to the beloved Gaius, whom I love in the truth.

Beloved, I pray that all may go well with you and that you may be in health; I know that it is well with your soul. For I greatly rejoiced when some of the brethren arrived and testified to the truth of your life, as indeed you do follow the truth. No greater joy can I have than this, to hear that my children follow the truth.

Beloved, it is a loyal thing you do when you render any service to the brethren, especially to strangers, who have testified to your love before the church. You will do well to send them on their journey as befits God's service. For they have set out for His sake and have accepted nothing from the heathen. So we ought to support such men, that we may be fellow workers in the truth.

I have written something to the church; but Diotrephes, who likes to put himself first, does not acknowledge my authority. So if I come, I will bring up what he is doing, prating against me with evil words. And not content with that, he refuses himself to welcome the brethren, and also stops those who want to welcome them, and puts them out of the church.

Beloved, do not imitate evil but imitate good. He who does good is of God; he who does evil has not seen God. Demetrius has testimony from every one, and from the truth itself; I testify to him too, and you know my testimony is true.

I had much to write to you, but I would rather not write with pen and ink; I hope to see you soon, and we will talk together face to face.

Peace be to you. The friends greet you. Greet the friends, every one of them."

This letter is even shorter in length than its predecessor – but it, too, teaches some very important truths! In a number of ways, it is complementary to II John.

In II John, the apostle had met some of the recipient's children and was able to provide an encouraging report; in III John, others had been able to provide John with an encouraging report about the recipient.

In II John, there is a warning against providing hospitality to false teachers; in III John, there is an encouragement to provide hospitality to faithful teachers.

In II John, the danger is from outwith the fellowship; in III John, the danger is from within the fellowship.

In II John, the apostle majors on doctrine, while not forgetting practical matters; in III John, he majors on practical matters, while not forgetting doctrine.

So what is the message of the letter?

The opening verses clearly show that John thought highly of Gaius. In each of his first two sentences, he refers to Gaius as *"beloved"*. Gaius is one who brought joy to the aged apostle – he prayed that Gaius' physical health be good; he had total confidence that he was well spiritually! One wonders if the reference, in this very personal note, to

"... *my children* ..." (v.4)

is a clue that he had been used by the Father to lead the younger man to faith in the Lord Jesus, the Christ – just as Paul refers to Timothy as his

"... *true child in the faith* ..." (I Tim.1:2),

and

> "... *my beloved child* ..." (II Tim.1:2).

However, what appears to have delighted John was Gaius' practice of hospitality. This is not a gift that all of the saints of God exercise! In the introduction to this letter, in the *Life Application Bible*, the contributor writes: "When company arrives at the door, with them comes the promise of soiled floors, dirty dishes, altered schedules, personal expense, and inconvenience. From sharing a meal to providing a bed, *hospitality* costs ... in time, energy, and money. But how we treat others reflects our true values. Do we see people as objects or inconveniences, or as unique creations of a loving God? And which is more important to God, a person or a carpet? Perhaps the most effective way to demonstrate God's values and Christ's love is to invite and welcome guests into our homes." (*in loc.*).

John recognised that, for Gaius, hospitality was an important function. The hospitality that he offered had, it would appear, become well-known. He was especially supportive of those who were

> "... *of the household of faith.*" (Gal.6:10),

and many had testified to his service and, we may be sure, generosity. Of course, in the early church, travelling preachers and teachers depended on such hospitality from their fellow-believers and, writes John, in providing it,

> "... *we may be fellow workers in the truth.*" (v.8).

F.F. Bruce makes the point that Gaius "... did not show hospitality in order to gain this renown – indeed, the renown probably meant that demand on his hospitality greatly increased – but thanks to their appreciative reports of his kindness, his example has been an encouragement too many others. His kindness was worthy of the God Whom he and they alike served; it was a reflection of God's own kindness (cf. II Sam 9:3, 'the kindness of God')." (*op.cit.*, p.150).

The suggestion is that a group of itinerant preachers, who had no visible means of support, rather looking to the Lord to meet their needs, and determined not to accept assistance from unbelievers, had gone out with the commendation of John and, perhaps, others in leadership positions. Some of them had reported back, favourably, on the hospitality offered by Gaius, and John was recognising this brother's contribution in the letter.

Although circumstances have changed over two millennia, it is still the case that a visiting preacher requires hospitality – whether that be a light lunch before his return home, or an overnight stay – and I can testify, personally, to the generosity of others when I have required such kindness to be shown to me.

Sadly, this is not the only reason for John's letter! Gaius was not the only person in the fellowship about whom the apostle had received reports! There was another member, named Diotrephes (the name means "nourished by Zeus" –

suggesting that he was a convert from heathenism), who appears to have been in a leadership position, but who was abusing that position.

> *"I have written something to the church; but Diotrephes, who likes to put himself first, does not acknowledge my authority. So if I come, I will bring up what he is doing, prating against me with evil words. And not content with that, he refuses himself to welcome the brethren, and also stops those who want to welcome them, and puts them out of the church."*

John refers to this man's presumption. He appears to have been an elder in the local fellowship of believers, but he acted like a dictator. He was filled with pride; one

> *"who likes to put himself first"*

Warren Wiersbe comments: "Instead of giving the pre-eminence to Jesus Christ (Col.1:18), he claimed it for himself. He had the final say-so about everything in the church, and his decisions were determined by one thing: 'What will this do for Diotrephes?' He was most unlike John the Baptist who said, 'He [Jesus Christ] must increase, but I must decrease.' (John 3:30).

The Greek verb indicates that it was the *constant attitude* of Diotrephes to promote himself." (*op. cit.*; *in loc*; *emphasis in original*).

Sadly, there are many modern versions of Diotrephes in our churches today – as well as in much of public life!

So what, specifically, had Diotrephes said/done that would bring such criticism from the aged apostle of love? Well, he rejected the authority of John within the church. Indeed, it would appear that John had already written to the church, but that Diotrephes had purloined the letter – if he hadn't actually destroyed it! Anyone who knows me well knows the great respect and love that I had (and have) for the late Rev. George B. Duncan. If, as a young minister, I had received a letter from Mr Duncan, on behalf of the church, I would have treasured such a document that would, I have no doubt at all, have been filled with wisdom born of so many years of faithful service. Yet here was a man who denied the fellowship words of wisdom from one who had walked, and worked, with the Lord Jesus Himself!

"It would seem that John had written to the church, but the letter was intercepted, and destroyed, by this man Diotrephes. He evidently was a man of considerable influence in the church, possibly with a following, and liked to control everything that went on in the church. It's possible that Diotrephes liked to monopolise the pulpit and that he felt threatened by the aged apostle. John may have written to the church, urging the willing reception of some of John's preacher friends, and that was the last thing Diotrephes wanted. Perhaps John had said something in the purloined letter about a proposed visit to the church, something Diotrephes wanted even less than visits from run-of-the-mill evangelists. It was a bold, if foolish, move to destroy an apostolic letter, and John was not about to let him get away with it. Hence, this letter to Gaius. Diotrephes would not be able to intercept *his* mail." (Phillips, p.222).

What a contrast between these two men! The commendation for Gaius is set against the condemnation of Diotrephes. The desire of Gaius to serve, is set against the personal ambition and masterful spirit of Diotrephes. The joy that Gaius brings to the apostle, is set against the pain caused by the "prating" of Diotrephes.

However, John also ensures that faithful, hospitable Gaius receives encouragement by sending him a like-minded colleague named Demetrius. One may assume, I believe, that Demetrius was, on this occasion, also acting as John's courier – bearing this letter to Gaius. The apostle would not have wished to, again, send it through the previously-used channels, as it would have likely suffered the same fate as the previous one! By sending it directly to a trusted brother, by the hand of a trusted brother, John was ensuring that Diotrephes would not get his hands on it.

It has been noted somewhere (sadly I don't have the details!) that the satan actually overreached himself by having the earlier letter destroyed or, at the very least, taken out of circulation. That letter had now been replaced by a Holy Spirit inspired letter that was to become one of the New Testament documents. This made it a permanent memorial to the triumph of the truth, and a warning to all who, like Diotrephes, are actually fighting against the God Who always wins; the God Who is working out His own plans and purposes, as year succeeds year.

As for Demetrius, it is clear that he had John's complete and unqualified endorsement. He

> *"... has testimony from every one, and from the truth itself; I testify to him too, and you know my testimony is true."* (v.12).

How kind of John to send such a brother to support Gaius, and strengthen him against any hostility that might emanate from Diotrephes.

The letter ends, in much the same way as II John, with the expressed desire that author and recipient might meet soon face-to-face. There is much else that John wishes to share with Gaius, but the spoken word is a much better medium of communication than the written word can ever be.

Then, there is a brief doxology wishing peace – even, we may safely assume, that peace that the beloved disciple would well remember being promised by the Saviour:

> *"Peace I leave with you; My peace I give to you; not as the world gives do I give to you. Let not your hearts be troubled, neither let them be afraid."* (John 14:27).

The double reference to

> "… *friends* …"

is not a general term for 'church members', but undoubtedly refers to those who, in both locations, were in sympathy with, and supported, the apostle.

The message of III John is, surely, simple and straightforward. It is that when the people of God love Him, and one another, and support those who minister to them, then God the Holy Spirit can work in that fellowship. However, when any one person becomes proud and overbearing then the Spirit is grieved and cannot bless. I have, myself, seen a work collapse because one person had, in my opinion, a spirit of control – much as that which appears to have been the case with Diotrephes. The fellowship may, for a time, appear to be operating 'successfully', but inwardly, there will not be the true unity of spirit, that comes from the Holy Spirit, and that makes for a healthy, growing, missionary church. There are today, as there were in John's time, those who are best described as

> "... *false prophets, who come to you in sheep's clothing but inwardly are ravenous wolves.*" (Matt.7:15).

May you and I never be found in their number. May we be, not like Diotrephes, but like Gaius and Demetrius, as God the Holy Spirit works in us, sanctifying us, until that Day when we shall be like Jesus (see I John 3:2).

Postscript!

If you found this book to be helpful, **PLEASE** leave a positive review on Amazon.

This is because Amazon promotes books based on the number of reviews an individual book receives. No reviews … the book will remain a secret.

Please remember that I receive **no** financial benefit from the sale of my books. **ALL** royalties are paid, **directly**, into the Bank Account of *Release International*, in support of the persecuted church.

If you are able to also recommend the book – <u>and the others in the series</u> – within your own Christian Fellowship, and among family and friends, encouraging them to purchase, this would be greatly appreciated. Perhaps your Amazon review could be reproduced in any regular newsletter, or the equivalent, that is published in the Fellowship!

Thank you, on behalf of those brothers and sisters who suffer for their faith in the Lord Jesus, in ways that most of us are truly unable to fully imagine, or understand.

About the author.

Brian Ross is an ordained minister of the Gospel, happily married and with two daughters, one of whom is herself married, and who has provided him with a grandson. He holds a number of academic qualifications, from a variety of establishments and in a variety of disciplines.

However, the qualification that is dearest to his heart is his Diploma of the Bible Training Institute – the result of his first foray into tertiary education, and the one that provided him with a solid evangelical base as he proceeded to achieve other academic success.

He has led a varied life, having commenced his adult work as a chef (including two years in the British Merchant Navy in which he was privileged to visit many parts of the world), continued as a parish minister in the Church of Scotland (Presbyterian), and completed it as Head of Religious and Moral Education in a Scottish State Secondary School. He has also been a regular presenter with two Christian radio stations; successfully presented a case at a two-part Industrial Tribunal; and twice stood (unsuccessfully!) as a candidate for the Scottish Christian Party at Holyrood and local elections. He spent the first three years of his 'retirement' as an active Chaplain to Strathclyde Police Force, deployed in 'N', and 'Q', Divisions, and at the Force Training and Recruitment Centre. He now exercises a ministry in south-west France – to both English-speaking and French-speaking groups.

His 'non-commercial' blog (www.crazyrev.blogspot.com) is, basically, a 'ministry blog', and he endeavours to post with a certain regularity! He contributes to various online fora and, of course, preaches whenever, and wherever, he is provided with the opportunity (all invitations prayerfully considered - author@minister.com).

GREAT WORDS OF THE FAITH
(from Faith to Eternity)

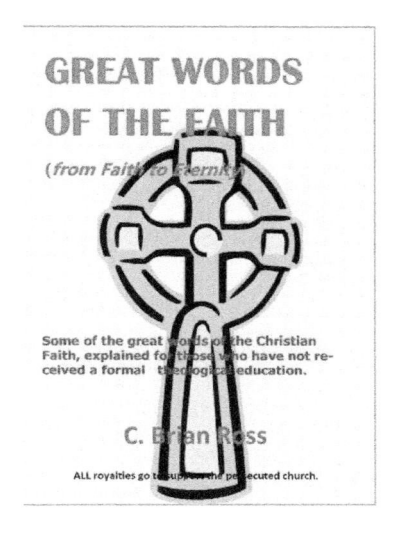

Some of the great words of the Christian Faith, explained for those who have not received a formal theological education.

C. Brian Ross

ALL royalties go to support the persecuted church.

Words that are frequently used by preachers and Bible teachers – but that many folk do not fully understand, are explained in simple terms.

Price (in U.K) £8.99

ISBN-13: 978-1540613547
ISBN-10: 1540613542

(Kindle e-book also available at £3.99)

Links available at

https://crazyrev.blogspot.com/

Twenty-five chapters and twenty-four Great Bible Words. Love, naturally, deserves two chapters. It is homely theology with notes of exhortation and encouragement. Full of quotable sayings, and supremely centred on Jesus Christ.

Rev. Dr. Derek Cook
Evangelist; Founder of *Christians in the Dordogne*

Brian presents his work as the long-term fruit of preaching and broadcasting. His aim is to give simple explanations of key Christian terms for the 'ordinary Joe' who has no formal theological training, but who would benefit from a clearer grasp of basic Christian concepts.

Rev. Dr. George J. Mitchell
Former Lecturer in Old Testament, The Bible Training Institute, Glasgow

In Great Words of the Faith, Brian Ross writes with simplicity on the right side of complexity. In so doing he enables us to understand difficult Christian terminology. Well done Brian! In simplicity lies beauty - something our minds can't resist.

Rev. Dr. Lawson Murray
President - Scripture Union Canada, Toronto

Foundations of the Faith.

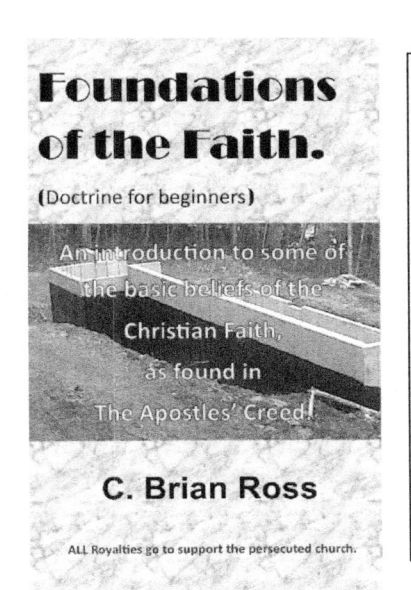

(Doctrine for beginners)

An introduction to some of the basic beliefs of the Christian Faith, as found in The Apostles' Creed.

C. Brian Ross

ALL Royalties go to support the persecuted church.

Getting to know some basic Christian teaching, using the wording of "The Apostles' Creed"

Price (in UK) £8.99
ISBN: 10: 151731206X
ISBN: 13: 978-1517312060

(Kindle e-book also available at £3.99)

Links available at

https://crazyrev.blogspot.com/

Following up his *"Great Words of the Faith"*, this is a timely piece of very accessible writing from a respected and experienced writer, teacher, and preacher. ... It is accessible, scholarly, personal, and full of scripture reference. The difficult issues are not skirted, but the fundamental truth of the Godhead is allowed to shine through.

Dr. Ken Cunningham, CBE, FRSA.

"Foundations of the Faith" should help all of those seeking to follow the Way of the Christ to do so more faithfully, and in an informed manner.
Rev. Derek Hughes, BSc., BD., DipEd.

Brian articulates what he believes with freshness and clarity. It is clear that for him, as for the distinguished Russian thinker, Berdyaev, Jesus is the starting point for learning Who God is, who we are, and what life is all about.

Very Rev. Dr. James A. Simpson, BSc., BD, STM

Printed in Great Britain
by Amazon